WRITTEN BY
YOLANDA RIDGE

ILLUSTRATED BY
DANE THIBEAULT

EVOLUTION UNDER PRESSURE

HOW WE CHANGE NATURE AND HOW NATURE CHANGES US

annick press

toronto · berkeley

For Oliver.
Thank you for helping me see the world in different ways and spreading optimism with every step you take. —Y.R.

To my mom and dad, who read to me when I was little and inspired me to never stop learning. —D.T.

Cover art by Dane Thibeault, designed by Maegan Fidelino based on a concept by Paul Covello
Interior design by Maegan Fidelino with art direction by Paul Covello

Edited by Kaela Cadieux
Line edited by Jennifer Foster
Copy edited by Becky Noelle
Proofread by Mary Ann Blair
Indexed by Wendy Thomas

Annick Press Ltd.

We acknowledge the support of the Canada Council for the Arts and the Ontario Arts Council, and the participation of the Government of Canada/la participation du gouvernement du Canada for our publishing activities.

Library and Archives Canada Cataloguing in Publication

Title: Evolution under pressure : how we change nature and how nature changes us / written by Yolanda Ridge ; illustrated by Dane Thibeault.
Names: Ridge, Yolanda, 1973- author. | Thibeault, Dane, illustrator.
Identifiers: Canadiana (print) 20220419965 | Canadiana (ebook) 20220419981 | ISBN 9781773217512 (hardcover) | ISBN 9781773217529 (softcover) | ISBN 9781773217536 (HTML) | ISBN 9781773217543 (PDF)
Subjects: LCSH: Nature—Effect of human beings on—Juvenile literature. | LCSH: Human beings—Effect of environment on—Juvenile literature. | LCSH: Human ecology—Juvenile literature. | LCSH: Sustainability—Juvenile literature.
Classification: LCC GF75 .R53 2023 | DDC j304.2—dc23

Published in the U.S.A. by Annick Press (U.S.) Ltd.
Distributed in Canada by University of Toronto Press.
Distributed in the U.S.A. by Publishers Group West.

Printed in China
annickpress.com
yolandaridge.com
danethibeaultart.com

Also available as an e-book. Please visit annickpress.com/ebooks for more details.

TABLE OF CONTENTS

INTRODUCTION

Have you ever looked in the mirror and wondered how you could possibly be related to a fish? Or a spider? Or even one of those blobby-looking amoebas you've seen swimming in pond water under the microscope?

Maybe you've watched your brother eat a banana and thought he looked a lot like a monkey? Or tried to follow your sister up a tree and wished you were more of a monkey yourself.

If every creature on Earth came from the same ancestor, why are we all so different? If we're all related to one another, why do just some of us thrive in the water? And how come only some of us can fly?

Each of us has our strengths—and weaknesses—which allow us to coexist within the same ecosystem. We can't all live in the trees, for example, or they would get crowded.

But only humans have figured out how to exist in almost every part of the world (even in space) by doing things like cutting down trees, growing crops, building cities, and inventing new ways to travel. We're the only ones who have altered our natural environment—on purpose—so it's better suited to *us*, rather than adapting to make us better suited to *it*. How does this affect plant and animal interaction? What impact does it have on our shared environment?

Understanding what evolution is—and isn't—is helpful in trying to answer these questions. The theory of evolution based on natural selection is a good place to start. But to really understand our role on Earth—and the effect humans have had on the evolution of all other species, including ourselves—we can also look at the idea of "not-so-natural selection."

What do animals like hornless rhinos, porky pigs, peppered moths, and anole lizards have in common? They're all good examples of not-so-natural selection, showing us how hunting, farming, inventing, and even moving to the city can have a huge impact on other animals.

None of these human activities are bad. We've always had an impact on other creatures, just like other creatures have an impact on us. The problem is, through not-so-natural selection, human activity has had a bigger impact on the environment and the creatures within it. We've changed the way the world works, interrupting the natural evolution of almost everything—and pretty quickly.

So what now? It's not like we can go back in time and "un-invent" things. And no one wants to go back to a time when we didn't live such a comfortable life.

How do we decrease the impact of human activity in a way that works for all creatures? How do we exist as part of the large tree of life without breaking too many branches?

To start, we'll take a quick trip back to the beginning and look at our own evolution. How did we start hunting, farming, and building factories and cities? How have these activities changed as humans have evolved?

Then we'll look at some specific characteristics—from horns and feet to appearance and attitude—to understand how not-so-natural selection has interrupted the evolution of certain animals.

Looking forward, we need to be more aware of where we've been and where we're going. It's not too late for humans to make choices that go beyond what's best for us and consider what's best for all of us, from amoebas, spiders, and moths to rhinos, lizards, pigs, and humans.

Humans might be significantly different than every other creature on the planet. But that doesn't mean we aren't dependent on our fellow creatures for survival.

Every living creature needs a healthy ecosystem to thrive. And as the animal with the largest impact, it's time for humans to ensure there's enough room—and trees—for everyone. Because it's about all of us—we're all interconnected.

NATURAL AND NOT-SO-NATURAL:
HOW SELECTION DRIVES EVOLUTION

Evolution is the gradual development of something simple into something more complex, like your science project changing from a page of notes into a multimedia presentation with slides, a light show, and an exploding volcano. Depending on who you ask—you, your teacher, or the classmate who got covered in a slimy mix of vinegar and baking soda—one is not necessarily better than the other, but one is definitely more complex. You could say the presentation evolved from the notes, just like the notes evolved from a blank piece of paper.

It's important to remember that the page of notes you worked so hard to create still exists. It could survive for a long time as is, in a box of school treasures, or it could evolve into something else—an essay, an exam study sheet, or the lining of your hamster's cage.

When we apply this idea of evolution to the development of life on Earth, it's often seen as a line with a beginning and an end: we started as apes/monkeys/fish (choose your ancestor) and ended up as perfectly evolved humans.

The problem? It's not that simple.

Things actually started way before apes, monkeys, and fish, with a stew of chemicals and molecules most of us would not consider "life." From there, single-celled organisms with the ability to reproduce emerged. As these single-celled organisms multiplied, changes occurred by random chance. This led to variation, eventually resulting in every organism we share the planet with today.

GENE MUTATIONS

Where do these random changes happen? In the genes—bits of instruction inside each cell that determine how a living creature will develop, function, and reproduce.

These instructions are made of DNA (deoxyribonucleic acid). Just like English is written using a code of twenty-six letters, genes are written with four letters—or bases—of DNA.

When a living creature reproduces, it passes on the genes in its instruction manual to the next generation by copying and packaging all those DNA bases into the nucleus of a new cell. This is how the next generation begins: with a single cell and a genetic instruction manual on how it can grow up to be just like its parent by making more and more cells.

But even the offspring of single-celled organisms can turn out different than their parent. Why? Mistakes are sometimes made in the copying of DNA. Like a spelling mistake, changing one of the letters in a gene's code—often called a mutation—can change how the instructions are read.

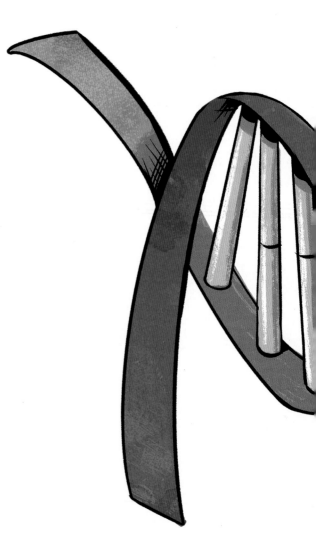

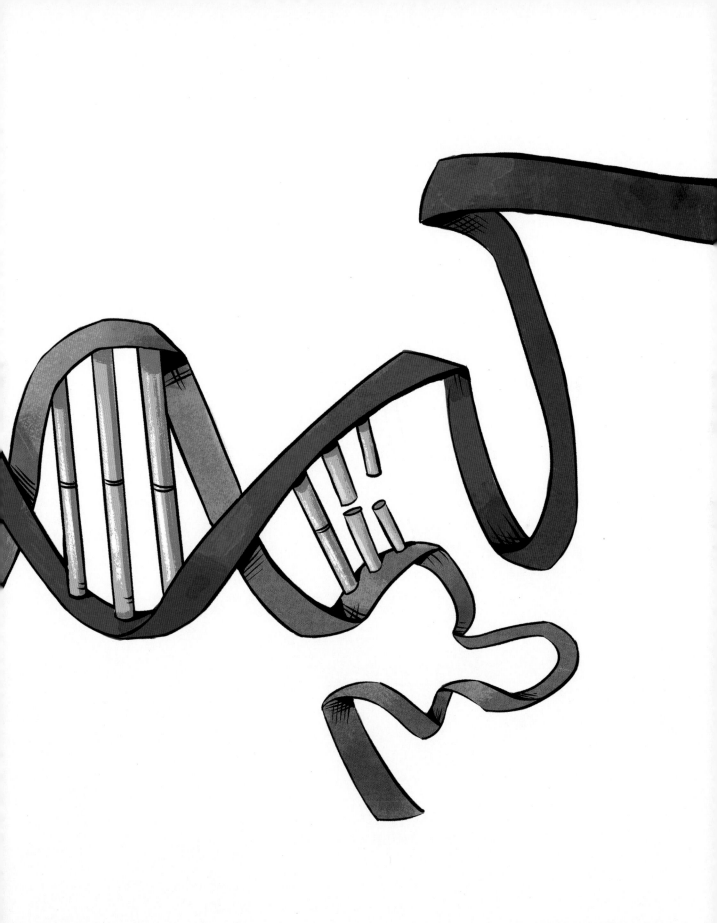

If you unraveled all the DNA in your cells, it would stretch to the moon and back six thousand times. That's a lot of letters to copy! And many mutations happen constantly, with different consequences. Some mutations are deadly, like changing "add vinegar to three teaspoons of baking soda" to "add poison to three teaspoons of baking soda," when building a model volcano. (A silly example, maybe, but remember: genes are written with only four bases of DNA, so little errors can create *big* changes.)

Most mutations have no effect on how the code is interpreted, like changing "three" to "3." But some gene mutations can actually change the instruction manual, creating something different, possibly even better, such as changing "add vinegar to three teaspoons of baking soda" to "add vinegar and red food coloring to three teaspoons of baking soda."

Like a spelling mistake, mutations are random. No one decides to add a spelling mistake to their essay, and creatures have no control over DNA copying mistakes in their genetic instruction manual.

What isn't random is what happens after a mistake is made. If the mistake makes something better, that set of instructions will likely be kept and followed over and over again until it becomes the new way of making a model volcano. But if a mistake makes something worse, that set of instructions will likely be tossed and forgotten.

Mutations that make a kid different from their parent in a way that helps them survive can become a permanent part of a new genetic instruction manual that's passed on to their kids. This creates the variation between generations, driving evolution.

THE TREE OF LIFE

Over time, this variation doesn't just create kids different than their parents. It also produces species of plants and animals totally different from one another.

From one basic instruction manual, all life on Earth evolved from a single-celled organism. And this evolution of life is more like a tree with branches than a straight line. From these single-celled organisms, different forms of life split off and then followed their own path. Plants formed their own big branch near the trunk, growing so large it was almost a second tree. Later, groups of animals as different as sea sponges (the kind that live in the sea, not in your sink) and insects branched off. Around 700 million years ago, another branch eventually produced creatures like starfish. Other branches appeared from this branch, including ones that led to vertebrates, then mammals, then people.

Hanging out at the end of all these branches are the organisms that have evolved most recently. They're not better or more powerful than creatures that evolved millions of years earlier, just the newest. Being new might make them more suited to our current world—like grandkids tend to be better at technology than grandparents—but it doesn't put them "on top."

The end of every branch in the evolution of life continues to grow. The random mutations that allowed humans to evolve from bacteria are still happening. So even though single-celled organisms are at the start of evolution (or close to it), there is no end point. At least not yet.

NATURAL SELECTION

Charles Darwin and Alfred Russel Wallace—naturalists who traveled the world researching and observing animals—were the first ones to come to the revolutionary conclusion that living things change over time in response to their environment. When they published their theory of natural selection, they weren't trying to explain where humans came from or how we climbed up the evolutionary tree. They were attempting to explain the similarities and differences between creatures living on different parts of Earth.

These scientists didn't know about genes and DNA (they were discovered later), but they observed that when animals reproduced, their offspring were sometimes different than the parents. These random changes were not always beneficial to the next generation.

But when a random change helped an organism survive, it was more likely to stick around and be copied. This is why natural selection is sometimes called "survival of the fittest." A creature that changes in a way that makes it more suited to its environment is more likely to survive long enough to reproduce and pass on their updated genetic instruction manual to the next generation.

For example, let's talk about the giraffe and how it might have developed a neck that looks better suited to mythology than life on Earth. During evolution, the ancestor of what we now call a giraffe had a baby with a longer neck than her parents because of a random gene mutation—let's call her Jandy. Luckily, Jandy was born in an environment with lots of tall trees, as well as with other animals that competed with the giraffe-like creatures for food.

Since Jandy's long neck allowed her to eat the leaves at the tops of trees, she had lots of food compared to her competitors. This made her extra healthy and able to produce many offspring. And Jandy's long neck gave both her and her calves a better view not just of the beautiful African landscape but also of dangerous predators with a craving for giraffe meat.

Both these advantages helped more of Jandy's family survive and then have more children with long necks or perhaps even longer necks than their parent. Evolution is a process that takes a long time—that neck doesn't grow overnight—so Jandy may have been the great-great-great-great-great-grandmother of the modern giraffe, which sports an even longer neck than she did.

It's important to remember that the environment and everything in it determine whether a new trait created by a random gene mutation will be carried into the next generation, or whether it will die out. If Jandy had been born in a land of shrubs or underwater, her long neck wouldn't have given her such a big advantage. It may have even been a disadvantage. The environment decides whether a new branch on the evolutionary tree will live or die.

NOT-SO-NATURAL SELECTION

Humans have influenced the evolution of other organisms for as long as we've been on the planet. Natural selection explains how plants and animals evolve through random gene mutations, helping them adapt to our interconnected environment. Not-so-natural selection, however, describes how plants and animals adapt to *us*.

If you've heard of the web of life (see below), you know all plants and animals have an influence over all other plants and animals within the same habitat. We know, for example, if the grass a deer typically dines on disappears—by a natural event such as disease or early frost or wildfire caused by lightning—the number of deer in that area will drastically decrease. With fewer deer, predators such as the mountain lion don't have much to dine on, so they're more likely to die. The only way to survive is by changing diets or moving.

Humans have this same type of influence over plants, animals, and even microorganisms like our single-celled ancestors. But there are several differences between natural selection caused by natural events and the not-so-natural human behaviors that influence evolution.

THE WEB OF LIFE

Imagine drawing lines between every plant, animal, and microorganism on Earth. This complex drawing represents the interconnectedness of all living things—each creature depends on every other creature for survival.

How does the "King of the Jungle" depend on a tiny microorganism?

A lion eats an antelope, which eats grass. Grass grows in soil containing nutrients from organic waste (including lion poop!), which relies on worms, bugs, and microorganisms to break it down.

Even though antelope may end up as a tasty lion treat, they rely on lions for the same reason—the grass antelope snack on grows with the help of lion poop containing different nutrients than the antelope's own poop. And in the end, they all rely on those poop-loving organisms to break it all down!

First, plants and nonhuman animals don't influence the evolution of other plants and animals *on purpose*. Humans are the only species that pick and choose which plants get to live through selective breeding and pest control. We are the only ones who've decided to grow specific plants in specific places and use animals for purposes other than survival.

Second, humans are the only species on Earth who make choices that have nothing to do with survival at all. When a mouse sneaks into your home to steal food, it's not doing it to win a bet or satisfy some curiosity about how humans live. The mouse just wants to survive and reproduce. It's not that simple for humans, though. As we have evolved, our motivations have also evolved far beyond survival.

Let's say you're chosen as a captain to build a team of classmates one by one, alternating your choices with the other captain. If all you cared about was winning, you'd pick the fastest or strongest person first. Or maybe the best leader. But because you're human, you won't necessarily do this—you might not pick the person most likely to help your team win.

Instead, you might pick someone because you like them—perhaps your best friend. Or because your teacher made you pick someone different. Why not choose the person who's going to help you win? Because people don't have to win to survive (although you may feel differently if you're super competitive). Survival's no longer the most important thing for people . . . not since survival became relatively easy for us.

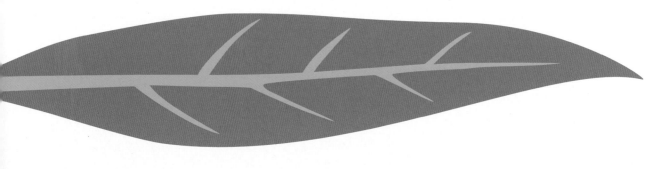

But as the human population grows, survival is becoming harder. And we're starting to realize just how much we rely on that web of life and the health of the planet to sustain us.

In the rest of this book, we'll look at the evolution of humans and how we've changed over the past five million years or so. As we've become stronger, smarter, and obsessed with stuff, we've had a bigger and bigger influence on the environment and all the organisms—from microbes to plants to other animals—we share it with. Through examples of not-so-natural selection, we'll discover just how resilient nature can be;

living things are constantly adapting to new environments and circumstances, and we've gotten pretty good at it too.

Still, there's a limit to how fast the natural world can change in response to human influence. The good news? While our power sometimes leads to damage we never intended or predicted, it can also be used to create positive change. Understanding how we've arrived at this place in history and exploring how we can move forward in ways that consider our place in the web of life are vital to making choices that support the surviving and thriving of all species—humans included.

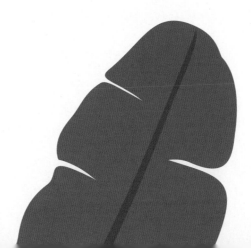

CHAPTER TWO:

HORNLESS: HOW HUNTING HURTS RHINOS

Just like it's hard to pinpoint the exact starting point of life on Earth, it's difficult to say when the first human-like creature branched off the evolutionary tree. Most scientists agree it happened around five to seven million years ago, which sounds like a really long time, but compared to other living creatures, we're the newbies.

Humans have never been the biggest, strongest, or fastest animals in the world. But thanks to those random genetic mutations covered in Chapter One, two big things happened to make our evolutionary path distinct:

1. Walking upright
2. Bigger brains

These human qualities made us different enough from our ancestors that we started following our own evolutionary path, while other primates continued on theirs. It didn't necessarily make us better than monkeys and apes, but it did make us suited to living in different environments—and in different ways.

HUNGRY HUMANS

Early humans collected food through hunting and gathering. Just like a cougar stalks and kills a deer, we might have captured small rodents or insects. And just like a squirrel, we probably collected nuts, seeds, and plants to satisfy our immediate hunger and keep us fed through the winter.

Walking on two feet allowed humans to use their hands. Our big brains discovered how to make and use more sophisticated tools, including weapons and traps, giving us a big advantage over our fellow creatures. Over millions of years, we got better at hunting and eventually started doing something other animals don't do—hunting for fun.

Our hunting practices have affected animals and the ecosystem we share with them in many ways. A good example comes from a mammal who hangs out quite close to us on the evolutionary tree: the rhinoceros.

DID YOU KNOW?

White rhinos can weigh up to 3,500 kg (7,700 pounds)—equivalent to two medium sized cars. (It's hard to believe they can get that big eating only leaves and grass!)

LIVING IN PEACE
WITH A POWERFUL BEAST

For most of our collective history, rhinos and humans have left each other alone. It's hard to take down a rhino, and most humans don't care much for rhino meat. And rhinos themselves don't like any meat at all. There have been some disputes over territory in the past—early humans probably didn't appreciate rhinos pooping next to their tent—but there was lots of room on Earth back then, especially in the parts of the world where rhinos roamed: Asia and Africa.

One of the most distinguishing characteristics of the rhinoceros (besides its massive size and armor-like skin) is its horn. Probably around the time Jandy started the trend of long giraffe necks, a rhino was accidently born with a horn, thanks to a random spelling mistake in its DNA. This gave the rhino, let's call him Bruno, a huge advantage over other male rhinos. Using his horn as a weapon, he could keep the others out of his territory, leaving the female rhinos with no one else to mate with. So Bruno had no trouble getting a mate. Or two. Eventually, Bruno became the father of many, many calves.

Since this accident happened because of a gene mutation, every one of Bruno's babies had a chance of inheriting the new "horn gene"—just like some of Jandy's babies inherited her long neck. Not every one of Bruno's kids would've been born with a horn, but those who were had advantages: a better ability to protect their territory and dig through compact, dry soil for edible roots, small plants, and water.

Through natural selection, more and more rhinos were born with horns because they were so beneficial to survival. Horns help rhinos so much that three of the five rhino species evolved to have two of them!

Fast-forward millions of years and, unfortunately, humans no longer leave rhinos alone. We're still not interested in rhino meat, but we are interested in something else: those magnificent horns.

DID YOU KNOW?

Black and white rhinos—the two African species—are actually gray.

WHY DO HUMANS NEED RHINO HORNS?

The short answer—we don't.

But rhino horn is good for making things: it's easy to carve and has a nice glossy color when polished. Ancient cultures made useful items like cups and dagger handles from it. Now it's used to make everything from belt buckles to door handles.

Ancient Greeks believed it could purify water, and Persians thought it could detect poisons.

Scientists think the Persians may have been onto something—the keratin in rhino horn (the same stuff that gives strength and structure to human fingernails, bird beaks, fish scales, and horse hooves)—may react with some poisons. But they have no explanation for why some ancient cultures started using it as medicine.

In the past, ground rhino horn has been used to

- lower fevers
- treat snakebite wounds, food poisoning, and possession by evil spirits
- cure headaches, hallucinations, high blood pressure, and typhoid

Today, people continue to use rhino horn as medicine, even without proof it works. Products containing rhino horn are sold as cancer treatments and even used as a sort of love potion in some parts of the world.

This huge desire for rhino horn has led to poaching—an illegal form of hunting. Since poachers are just after the rhino's horn, they don't usually shoot to kill. Instead, they shoot a type of poison dart that tranquilizes the animal (puts it to sleep). Sadly, a lot of rhinos die from the wounds left behind after the poacher cuts off their horn.

Even though rhino hunting is illegal in most countries, close to 10,000 African rhinos have been killed by poachers in the last ten years—that's three rhinos every day! Three of the five rhino species are now considered critically endangered, meaning they're at extremely high risk of disappearing from the wild. The Javan rhino, in Indonesia, is one of the rarest large mammals on Earth with fewer than eighty left in the wild.

HORNLESS RHINOS

Thankfully, nature is fighting back against poaching, and here's where not-so-natural selection comes in. If a rhino has no horn, there's no reason for a poacher to hunt it, right? Thanks to a random spelling mistake that happened when the DNA of one rhino's instruction manual was copied, that's exactly what happened.

And this mistake happened at just the right time and place. If it had happened earlier—when humans weren't interested in rhino horn—the rhino wouldn't have had an advantage. The hornless rhino would've had a disadvantage over rhinos with horns because it couldn't protect its territory or dig for food and water. But with poachers, the rhino accidently born without horns became the lucky one—like winning the lottery.

Having horns went from being an advantage to a disadvantage because rhinos now live in a different environment—one that contains poachers. So rhinos have started climbing back down the evolutionary tree as a way of adapting—not to *nature* but to *us*.

DID YOU KNOW?

The word rhinoceros means "nose horn." Javan and Indian rhinos have one horn. The white, black, and Sumatran rhinos have two.

As a result, most hornless rhinos will live longer than their horned relatives. And what will a hornless rhino do with all that extra time? Have more kids, of course!

Genetically speaking, rhinos without horns are not only more likely to reproduce, but they're also more likely to have baby rhinos without horns. Over time, there will be more rhinos without horns than with horns because their environment has changed to include a new predator who can't be fought off with those handy horns: humans.

Bad news for the poachers.
Good news for the rhinos.

Unfortunately, it's not quite that simple.

A rhino has horns for defending its territory and getting food and water for survival. Not having horns might save the rhino from poachers but also makes it more difficult to eat, reproduce, and fight off other competitors.

Because of the climate crisis (see "Change versus Crisis"), rhinos are now dealing with more environmental changes. There's less rain where they live. In some cases, this has led to droughts (periods of dry weather that cause water shortages and crop damage). These severe climate conditions make it very difficult for rhinos,

CHANGE VERSUS CRISIS

Earth's climate normally changes slowly over time, but it's now changing faster than ever. Our planet has warmed up ten times faster over the last century than at any other time.

Most scientists agree this rapid change is related to human activities, including

- burning fossil fuels (coal, oil, and gas) to make electricity and fuel our cars and planes
- cutting down forests to make houses, factories, and farms

These activities lead to an increase in greenhouse gases like carbon dioxide and methane, which trap warm air in the planet's atmosphere and change water and air currents, creating more storms and unpredictable weather.

Earth can only handle so much change at once, and things are changing so fast now that many consider us in a climate crisis.

which will need every tool they have—including those horns—to dig through dirt for water and food.

Some rhinos have survived climate change before. But not all. The woolly rhino (friend of the woolly mammoth and saber-toothed tiger) went extinct after a brief warming period near the end of the last ice age. Sea levels rose as ice melted, changing the woolly rhinos' habitat and food resources so much they couldn't survive. Our fifteen-thousand-year-old ancestors were alive then—hunting in Siberia where the woolly rhinos lived—but they were only hunting for their own survival; they weren't burning the fossil fuels responsible for today's climate crisis.

RHINO RELATIVES

Rhinos aren't the only animal evolving in the fight against poaching. Elephants—hunted for their ivory tusks—are also becoming tuskless, thanks to not-so-natural selection. Here's some proof:

- In one of Zambia's national parks, female elephants born without tusks increased from 10 percent to almost 40 percent in just twenty years.
- In Sri Lanka, where there's been a lot of poaching, less than 5 percent of male Asian elephants now have tusks.

Estimates say between twenty-five and thirty thousand African elephants are killed by poachers yearly despite an ivory ban. So being tuskless may save the African elephant from becoming endangered, like the rhino, but not without a cost. Like the rhino's horn, elephant tusks aren't just there to make the elephant look good. They're used as weapons during mating season and as tools to dig for water and roots.

The same is true for bighorn sheep in North America, which face a threat similar to their African cousins. Bighorn sheep need the horns they're named after for fighting for female attention and guarding their territory. Unfortunately, having horns that are attractive to trophy hunters is proving to be a bigger risk than not being able to butt heads with other males.

EVOLUTION UNDER PRESSURE

Whether today's rhinos can survive both poaching and human-caused climate change—without horns—remains to be seen. These magnificent creatures have shown they can adapt even when their evolution is impacted by humans, but if we keep pushing too far, too fast, there's a chance they could go the way of the woolly rhino and disappear.

Some people think losing one animal—like the bighorn sheep, for example—is no big deal. But remember, every animal exists within the larger web of life. There are predators—like cougars, wolves, bobcats, coyotes, and even golden eagles—that rely on a belly full of sheep to get through the winter. And even though large herbivores eat a lot of vegetation, they also help things grow by fertilizing plants with their poop, pruning shrubs when they nibble on shoots and leaves, and tilling the land when they dig through dirt with their horns.

Humans need to recognize the impact we have when we hunt. There's still time to change our relationship with rhinos and other animals affected by our advanced hunting practices—as long as we start hunting more responsibly.

WHAT DO WE DO NOW?

Hunting rhinos for their horns is illegal in most places—that's why it's called poaching. But there's more that humans can do to help the rhino.

We can make hunting rhinos illegal in every country and make the penalties higher for lawbreakers. And we can get better at catching them.

For many years, we've tried to catch poachers the same way poachers catch rhinos: by tracking them down. Now these efforts are getting a high-tech boost. Here's some of the current technology being used to predict, locate, track, and catch suspected poachers:

- drones take photos, make videos, and create 2D and 3D maps of large areas where rhinos roam
- forensic DNA tracking locates poachers after illegal rhino horn has been confiscated
- alarm fences around wildlife reserves send a text message to rangers when compromised
- hidden cameras triggered by the movement of large animals send images directly to anti-poaching teams
- GPS collars track the location and movement of rhino herds

Poachers have access to some of this technology, too, which is why we need to consider another approach as well. Instead of trying to catch poachers, we can take away their desire to poach by destroying the market for rhino horn. Think of it this way: if a store sells shoes, and no one wants those shoes, the store goes out of business because there's no market for their product. If a poacher can't sell rhino horn, they will stop killing rhinos to get it.

Conservationists have tried to destroy the market for rhino horn in several ways:

- educating the public on what rhino horn can and can't do
- selling fake rhino horn at a lower price than the real stuff
- implanting GPS microchips (so the horns can be tracked whether they are on the rhino or not) and pink dye (because bright pink horns are hard to sell) into horns through a process that's completely painless for the rhino

It costs a lot of money to do some of these things. And capturing rhinos to implant chips or add collars can be dangerous to both the rhino and the person trying to protect them.

No solution is perfect, but trying to protect the rhino still makes sense. Why? Here are a few good reasons:

- Rhinos help the environment by acting as lawnmowers and gardeners. Without them grazing, digging, and pooping all over the savanna, some grass species would disappear. Shrubs and small trees would also suffer without rhinos keeping them pruned.
- Rhinos are considered a keystone species in the web of life. The work they do as gardeners ensures that other herbivores like zebras, gazelles, and antelope have enough to eat. Healthy vegetation also gives carnivores like lions and leopards places to hide while hunting for their lunch.
- Rhino herds are like a human family. People who work with rhinos say they're sensitive, smart, playful, and deeply loyal to their loved ones.
- Rhinos can help people without sacrificing their horns. Safaris—where tourists pay big bucks to view animals in their natural habitat—bring much needed income to countries in places like Africa and much joy to the people who are fortunate enough to see rhinos in the wild.

It's unclear how much each effort to stop rhino poaching is working. But there's some evidence fewer rhinos are being killed every year. In 2021, the number of African rhinos poached dropped by almost 800 compared to five years earlier.

Animals like the rhino still need help, though, and there are little things you can do to make a difference. You can join an organization like Save the Rhino or donate money to the Rhino Rescue Project. And you can also exercise your purchasing power by making sure you know what's in the products you buy. A real ivory necklace, for example, is made from elephant tusk—something you might not want hanging around your neck once you know where it's from and how it was obtained.

LOOKING FORWARD

If you think some of the things being done to stop poachers—alarms, fences, hidden cameras, drones, and guns—sound like something from a war movie or a crime show, you're not wrong. Some say the battle between conservationists and poachers is a war that cannot be won. And like a war, it has casualties on both sides.

In the long term, society needs to look at the underlying cause of poaching. Most thieves don't steal for fun but because they need money to survive. Most poachers aren't killing rhinos because they want to. They're doing it because they need to sell rhino horn so they can provide shelter and food for their families.

For this reason, funding education programs and seeking input from local communities on how to reduce both the need to make a living through poaching and the market for rhino horn are vitally important. It might take a long time, but reducing inequality in the

world is also something humans need to work toward. We need to eliminate poverty and make sure people doing things like poaching for a living have other options to support themselves. This way, we can all work together to protect the rhino.

Beyond saving the rhino, humans need to think more about why and how we hunt all animals. That doesn't necessarily mean we shouldn't hunt at all. When hunting is done right—following guidelines put out by conservation groups and government organizations—it can be an important part of keeping animal populations under control.

There are also people in many parts of the world who still hunt for food. Hunting is an important aspect of many Indigenous cultures and provides more than just nourishment; it can also be part of religious ceremonies, societal traditions, and a healthy lifestyle.

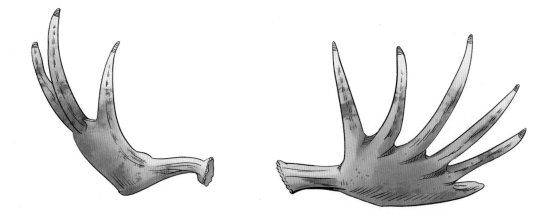

So what does it mean to "hunt right"? This is a difficult question. To get answers, we need to collect information and collaborate with people like

- mathematicians and ecologists who calculate how many animals are needed to sustain a healthy population and make models on how hunting will affect those numbers in the future
- scientists who study how each specific animal affects all the other plants and animals in the ecosystem
- individuals who live in the same habitat as the animals and understand their interconnectedness
- Indigenous people who live in harmony with land and animals (see "Land Guardians")
- hunters who appreciate how modern technology and the rising human population increases how many animals can be hunted and the need to limit those numbers
- governments and conservation groups who assess the impact of these limits on different communities and cultures

There's no reason hunting can't continue if it's done responsibly. To achieve this, we must pay attention not only to the impact we're having on one individual animal but also how we're affecting the ecosystem as a whole. By limiting how much animals must respond to not-so-natural selection, they will be better able to adapt to the changing climate through evolution by natural selection—something that's not just good for them but also the entire web of life.

MAKING A DIFFERENCE:
LAND GUARDIANS

The Dane Nan Yế Dāh Kaska Land Guardian Program started in 2015 from concerns about moose poaching within the traditional territory of the Kaska Dena First Nations in British Columbia, Yukon, and the Northwest Territories. "We'd find a moose shot and the antlers taken off or sometimes [the moose was] just shot and left," says Land Guardian coordinator Tanya Ball.

Land Guardians—including Elders, Indigenous hunters, and youth—use traditional knowledge and science to monitor everything from wildlife health to water quality to land use. With special apps and mapping software, they monitor many animals, focusing on moose and sustainable hunting. "First Nations rely on moose for sustenance. And we use all parts of the animal, from guts to ribs."

Information such as how many babies each mama moose has (the calf to cow ratio) and how things are changing in response to climate and environmental changes are important to the long-term health of moose and Indigenous people. Land Guardians also serve as the "eyes and ears" of the territory to make sure hunting is done sustainably.

"We don't have control over who gets a license to hunt in our territory, but we do work with government, and we've built some great relationships with guide outfitters." Tanya gives one example of an outfitter—who brings tourists into the area to hunt—that donated moose, caribou, and mountain goat meat to a community freezer in Lower Post, BC, feeding twenty-seven homes in one year.

This program is one of over fifty similar programs across Canada. Youth are encouraged to participate and get to do cool stuff like riding in helicopters and building emergency shelters.

"Indigenous Guardian programs strengthen our communities. They create jobs, lower crime rates, and improve public health. But most importantly, they inspire our young people," says Valérie Courtois, director of the Indigenous Leadership Initiative. "They connect them to the land and their elders. They give them professional training tied to their language and culture. That offers hope that can combat the despair so many Indigenous youth feel today."

CHAPTER THREE

PLEASANT PORK: HOW FARMING PICKS PIGS

Hunting with traps and weapons made survival and moving around easier for early humans.

By this time—thousands of years ago—big-brained *Homo sapiens* had learned how to cooperate and make plans. We became curious, using our knowledge to seek out new lands. From Africa, we spread to what is now Europe and Eurasia. Through teamwork, we learned to make boats for crossing large bodies of water, settling in places like New Guinea and Australia.

Following big animals and hunting on the move, we found good places to live as both climate and geography changed over time. It also led to the ethnic diversity found on Earth today.

It wasn't so great for everyone else on the tree of life, however. Our arrival affected the world in two big ways:

1. *Homo sapiens* became the only survivor of the hominin species.

2. Many plants and animals went extinct (see "The Sixth Extinction" on page 62).

The animals we encountered as we wandered through the continents had never seen a human before and needed time to evolve and change in response to human hunters who, along with spears, flint weapons, and bows and arrows, had also learned to control fire.

Busy thinking of ourselves and our own survival, we didn't really notice our impact on others. Ready to settle down, we set our big brains on a new task: figuring out how to grow crops and keep animals in captivity.

DOWN ON THE FARM

People didn't record everything on their phones back then, so it's hard to know exactly how or why we settled on the farm. We do know it happened in different parts of the world at roughly the same time, based on archeological evidence of small, permanent settlements. By digging up old bones and stone tools, scientists have figured out these early settlers planted seeds and captured animals to fill the barn.

Farming might seem old school, but since hunting and gathering was the only form of subsistence for most of human history, this behavior change was revolutionary. Until we moved to the farm, humans lived much like other animals—adapting to the environment. Thanks to agriculture and the domestication of plants and animals (see "Domesticating versus Taming"), things reversed, and we started drastically transforming the environment to suit us instead.

DID YOU KNOW?

Pig tails are a common menu item in many parts of the world—added to soups, cooked twice so they're extra crispy, or eaten in sandwiches.

We've been doing it ever since. As our methods have become more sophisticated, our impact on the world has become larger and more complicated. One food that shows how much agriculture has evolved since we planted the first wheat seed is something you might've had for breakfast. Or maybe you had it for dessert since this food is eaten with everything from pancakes and eggs to ice cream and fudge. Yep—we're talking about bacon and the animal we have to thank for providing it.

DOMESTICATING VERSUS TAMING

These two terms are often used interchangeably. But there's a big difference.

Domestication happens to a whole species as a result of controlled breeding of a wild plant or animal—a process that changes their genetic instruction manual. If a domestic pig has a baby, that piglet will also be domestic.

Taming happens when an individual member of a species learns to live with humans and behave the way people want them to. If a zoo lion has a baby that's immediately released into the wild, it will not be tame.

SWEET
SWINE

If you've ever met a wild pig, you know they can be very unfriendly. But that didn't stop our ancestors from hunting them and figuring out how to keep some for future dining.

Wild pigs are hard to hunt—they're smart, strong, and fight viciously when cornered, making them difficult to keep in captivity as well. So people started favoring the more pleasant pigs.

The first farmers didn't know about natural and not-so-natural selection, but they did what made sense: if you have two pigs in a pen and you need something for dinner, you eat the one that's not-so-nice. The better a pig behaved, the longer it was likely to stick around.

After a while, our farming ancestors figured out that female pigs were good for something besides eating—breeding. Farmers became matchmakers, setting up domestic females with wild males and hoping for a love connection.

DID YOU KNOW?

The expression "eat like a pig" comes from the fact that pigs are messy eaters, but they don't "pig out." When it comes to overeating, they show more restraint than most humans.

It wasn't long before the barnyard was full of piglets. Now farmers could keep more and more pigs without having to hunt. And since mama pig was chosen for breeding rather than eating because of her pleasing disposition, her piglets were more likely to be sweet-mannered swine—like everything else, at least part of our personality is coded in the genes. Female pigs have twelve to fourteen piglets in every litter, and it was up to the farmer to choose which ones got eaten and which ones were chosen for mating.

Over time, the easiest pigs to have around were the ones who had babies. And since there were more of them, both parents could be chosen based on their winning personalities. There was no need to add any more wild pig genes to the mix.

This cycle of not-so-natural selection—pigs evolving to adapt to farm life—has gone on for twelve thousand years. The pigs you see on the farm today are nothing like their wild cousins.

FIT FOR THE FARM

Many large mammals have roamed the Earth, but only a few—like goats, cows, and horses—have been domesticated. What makes a large mammal suited to farm life?

- having a hierarchy (if they're used to having a boss, they won't mind a farmer ordering them around)
- being social (so they can live in a group)
- reproducing quickly (so farmers don't have to wait too long for them to grow up)
- being vegetarian (because grass is cheaper than meat!)

PIG TAILS

Modern farmers still choose which pigs to breed and which pigs to eat based on characteristics like

- appearance (we prefer smooth pink pigs to brown and hairy ones)
- fat to muscle ratio (the more body fat, the better the bacon)
- disposition (not getting vicious when backed into a barn corner)

Today, we don't just decide which genes get passed on to the next generation by what's now called selective breeding. We also do it by changing the genes directly.

Before we get too ahead of ourselves, though, let's go back to the bottom. Let's talk tail.

Ever wondered what a pig tail is for—besides eating? Like a lot of animals, pigs use their tails as a way of communicating.

Warthogs, for example, have straight tails that go up like a flag when they run. Scientists think a mama warthog does this as a way of keeping her young behind her in single file. Through natural selection, warthogs with longer, straighter tails probably had an advantage because they were better able to keep their offspring safe and in line.

Through not-so-natural selection, domestic pigs have ended up with curly tails. Maybe curly tails are more fashionable on the farm. Or the trait was selected for breeding because shorter, curlier tails were less likely to get bitten by other pigs in crowded barnyards.

Either way, domestic pigs still used their tails to communicate. Until we started getting rid of them altogether.

DID YOU KNOW?

Wild pigs forage for mushrooms, grass, acorns, and roots and chow down on nuts, fruit, worms, insects, eggs, and small birds and mammals.

AGROTECHNOLOGY

Where did tailless pigs come from? Unlike the random mutation that made Bruno more likely to survive in a world with poachers, pigs have lost their tails because of direct human intervention.

Waiting for random mutations to make a creature better suited to us—then relying on that creature to reproduce—takes too long for us modern humans, who live in a world where everything's instant. To shorten the process, farmers started clipping off the pig's tail as soon as it was born.

This isn't like clipping your fingernails or cutting your hair. It hurts the pig, making it dangerous for the farmer. So smart humans are figuring out how to change the pig's genetic instruction manual instead.

In the last twenty years or so, scientists have developed a way of changing specific genes in many living organisms. By mutating tail-growing genes very early in development, a pig can be born without a tail because the instructions aren't followed.

The process isn't that much different than searching through a Word document to find a certain word or sentence so you can change it or delete it, which is why it's called gene editing. Unlike natural selection, though, there's nothing random about it. Scientists know exactly what DNA sequence they're looking for and make changes based on what instructions they want in the manual.

If the instruction manual is changed/edited during the early stages of pig development, the pig will be born without a tail. Do this to enough pigs, and the tailless trait will be inherited by future generations, and voilà—no more tails.

Gene-editing technology is getting better all the time, and that's probably a good thing for both farmer and pig. Domestic pigs have other ways to communicate, and they probably don't miss having to choose between a painful birthday clipping or a lifetime of having their tail bitten by barnyard buddies.

Agrotechnology—technology used to improve agriculture quantity, efficiency, and profitability—hasn't stopped at pig tails, however. With a small change to a different section of the genetic instruction manual, pigs can become resistant to disease. Gene editing can also create micropig pets and pigs with organs suitable for human transplant.

FEEDING THE PIGS

To feed us, pigs must be fed. Without crops—from wheat to beets—there's no bacon.

These crops have also been affected by not-so-natural selection. For plants, evolution happens quicker because their genetic instruction manual is different and they produce more offspring. You might not think of a plant as reproducing, but when you cut open a tomato, it's usually packed with seeds. Every seed can make a seedling, and that's just from one tomato growing on a plant that produces many more.

Early farmers didn't choose crops based on their temperament, however, probably because there's no such thing as a grumpy carrot. Instead, they chose seeds from plants based on things like

- yield (the amount of food produced from each plant)
- shelf life (how well the fruit, vegetable, or grain can be stored or shipped)
- taste
- appearance (like with pigs, the prettier the better)

With gene editing, we're now creating crops that will grow how, where, and when we want. It's also being used to make different changes to the plant's instruction manual, depending on whether we're growing a crop to feed the pigs or ourselves or produce biofuels like ethanol made from corn.

We can produce everything from pesticide- and pest-resistant banana plants to rice that can grow in a drought. And we're even "undoing" some of the evolutionary changes caused by early plant domestication, recreating more diverse and healthy varieties of our favorite fruits and vegetables.

DID YOU KNOW?

Farm pigs mostly eat leftover vegetables and hay. For treats, they can be served eggs and cheese but never raw meat.

EVOLUTION UNDER PRESSURE

Pigs evolved to have long tails and quick tempers. Both things helped them survive in the wild: their temper made them harder to hunt, and their tail kept young pigs in line.

Humans interrupted, and wild pigs became not-so-wild. Farmers wanted pigs that could get along with other barnyard animals. And we didn't like the pig's tail—a pain for farmer and pig.

Instead of waiting around for natural selection, we figured out how to make pigs better suited to the farm.

We did the same thing with other livestock and the crops we grow to feed them. Through selective breeding, we've interrupted the evolution of everything in the barnyard and the fields, creating a whole new web of life: one that exists in the not-so-natural environment we created for it—the farm.

As humans have evolved, we've figured out how to make changes to the genetic instruction manual directly. Using gene-editing technology, we can now use not-so-natural selection to control the evolution of every plant and animal on the planet—including ourselves.

WHAT DO WE DO NOW?

Now you might be thinking agriculture has become too complicated. Maybe we should go back to hunting and gathering? Or turn back the clock to a time when we weren't making such drastic changes to the plants and animals that feed us?

Unfortunately, it's not that easy. Without agriculture, the human population would not be as large as it is today because we wouldn't be able to feed everyone. And we wouldn't have the lifestyle most of us are lucky to enjoy.

That doesn't mean we can't change the way things happen on the farm. In some cases, that means going back to the basics. You could get involved by having your own backyard garden where you do stuff like

- save seeds
- grow food suited to your area in the right season
- plant things that grow well together to reduce the need for pesticides
- use compost to limit using chemical fertilizers

Most of us don't have enough room to keep a pet pig. But you might be able to keep backyard chickens that provide eggs and perhaps meat. Or maybe you can find a neighbor with chickens, which, at certain times of the year, will often produce more eggs than their owner can eat—no matter how much they like quiche!

Even if you do all these things, you must still rely on commercial farmers for some of your food, especially if you live in an area with harsh winters not suitable for growing anything but snow sculptures. But there are things you can do at the grocery store:

- buy less meat (The animals we eat are often treated poorly, and producing their food has a big environmental impact.)
- choose sustainably grown food (Do you really need something grown somewhere that used to be a rainforest?)
- pick fruits and vegetables grown closer to home
- join a local farm collective (see "Grow Dat!" on page 59)

There's still a limit to how much this will help, however. It's difficult for strict organic farming to sustain our growing population because it generally requires more land to produce the same amount of food. And some parts of the world can't afford organic pesticides and fertilizers, which tend to be more expensive. In those countries with organic farming, a lot of people can't pay the higher price of organically produced food.

Most people think that at this point in our own evolution, we must rely on technology to improve commercial food production. Instead of forcing plants and animals to evolve the way we want them to, we could give the plant or animal exactly what it needs to grow well. One example of this is a lettuce-bot. Yes—a robot! Actually, it's a group of robots pulled behind a tractor. As they go through the field, they can

- test the soil's nutrients and fertilize each plant accordingly
- test the soil's moisture and provide the exact amount of water the plant needs
- pull out individual weeds using technology like facial recognition
- determine when a plant should be harvested

Lettuce-bots aren't just cool—they're a portal to the past. We've always selected plants and animals to suit us. But it's only in the last century we've stopped giving them the individual care and attention they deserve. We can have a big impact by using technology to create the environment they need to grow well.

LOOKING FORWARD

People have different opinions on how animals should be treated and whether it's good to eat food from an animal or a plant with genes that have been changed directly or indirectly. In reality, though, the genetic instruction manual of almost everything we buy in the grocery store has been selected, modified, or edited to suit life on the farm through not-so-natural selection.

In the same way hunting is not all bad, gene editing and other types of agrotechnology are not all bad. They may even be necessary. Without them, we're unlikely to be able to feed the world's ballooning population. Especially as growing conditions become more difficult due to extreme weather events such as drought.

The problem with forcing plants and animals to evolve in ways that make it easier to farm them is that there's potentially no limit. To make informed choices about what are good and bad uses of agrotechnology, we need to consider the following:

Why are we doing it? Many of the ways we've forced pigs to evolve have been for our benefit, not the pig's. Tailless, pest-free pigs can be packed into a dirty barn with no room to move, allowing farmers to make more money, but at what cost to the pig?

Is it good for us? How an animal's raised can have a big impact on the food it provides. A domestic chicken allowed to roam in the pasture produces more healthy meat and eggs than a caged one. Does a pig not worried about having its tail bitten off produce better pork?

What impact will it have on other plants and animals? When a happy, gene-edited pig escapes the pen, it's unlikely to survive in the wild. If it does, it could mate with a wild pig, starting a not-so-natural selection process that dilutes the wild pig's survival genes and replaces them with pig genes more suited to the farm. Could something like that make the wild pig population extinct? How would this affect that pig's ecosystem, including the plants in its web of life?

What impact will it have on the environment? Gene-edited plants can be good for the environment if they reduce the use of things like pesticides, fertilizer, or water. Making a plant resistant to pesticides so it can be used to eliminate weeds may be not-so-great, however. And since plant seeds escape the farm a lot easier than animals, the changes we make to plant genes are more likely to "flow" into the wild population. How could this impact wild plants, the animals who eat them, and the environment they live in?

These are important—but hard—questions to answer. We must make sure we know what we're doing, especially when it comes to messing with the instruction manual of another creature. We've already forced plants and animals to adapt to human agriculture through not-so-natural selection. If we're going to continue interrupting the evolution of livestock and crops through increasingly advanced agrotechnology, we should also know how to fix things if something goes wrong.

It's not just the farmers or the politicians who need to make these kinds of decisions. Anyone who eats will have a say in how agrotechnology is used in the future. It will also be up to all of us to make sure the food we produce gets distributed evenly worldwide.

On the evolutionary tree, the distance between pigs and humans might seem huge. But we actually share the same branch. And the future of the human species is as dependent on the future of domestic creatures like the pig as they are on us—because we're all dependent on each other.

MAKING A DIFFERENCE:
GROW DAT!

Grow Dat Youth Farm in New Orleans, Louisiana, aims to do two things:

1. Give youth living in poverty access to fresh food.
2. Provide unique opportunities for high school students to develop leadership skills and spark community change.

Kayla White joined Grow Dat when she was sixteen. She's now a Crew Leader known as K-White. "The youth farm benefits the community because people know where their foods are coming from," she says. "It is more affordable and tasty. Having a farm in your neighborhood gives you a new look on what's being offered."

Kayla says the most important thing about growing food sustainably is taking care of the soil. "When you protect the soil, the better and stronger the produce becomes."

Each year, she helps grow 15,875 kg (35,000 pounds) of food, a third of which is donated to people in need. "Food justice is everyone having equal access to fresh foods [and] pricing fresh food at an affordable rate, so people from all socioeconomic statuses achieve great health."

Ethnicity and gender equity are also important to Ancestral Acres Farm and Garden, an initiative by Seeding Sovereignty. Through BIPOC (Black, Indigenous, People of Color) stewardship, the farm aims to grow food for the community and save seeds for future farming projects. Land Steward Mayam Garris started the farm in the Indigenous Tiwa Territory of Albuquerque, New Mexico. "Being in a lot of rural areas as a Black queer farmer—there's not too many of us in rural areas—I learned a lot about how to hold myself, love myself . . . and keep [going] when I start to feel lonely," they say. "Ultimately, I want to get the youth involved. I want to learn, teach, and listen to the youth."

K-White agrees with Mayam on the importance of getting people involved in farming at a young age. "I've learned things about the land, food security, mental and physical health, and being the best person I can be. Grow Dat taught me about growing my own vegetables and how to cook, so I can be physically healthy."

CHAPTER FOUR:

CAMOUFLAGE: HOW POLLUTION COLORS MOTHS

We were happy on the farm for thousands of years. It was hard work since everything had to be done by hand. Many people also think it led to a decline in nutrition and an increase in disease. But controlling our environment seemed worth it. We had food in the cupboard and a warm bed for sleeping.

With more food and better shelter, the population grew. People got together to share knowledge and make trades. This led to two major advancements:

1. New tools like wooden, horse-drawn plows
2. Machines powered by steam engines

We get the term "technology" from these inventions, although none of them were nearly as small and powerful as the phones we carry with us today. A steam engine definitely didn't fit into anyone's pocket!

When technology and industry (the production of stuff like food and clothes) came together—about 200 years ago—it resulted in what's now called the industrial revolution.

The industrial revolution changed human society faster than any other event in our history. It resulted in the production of many things we still have today—including pollution.

MADE BY MACHINE

The ability to make things by machine changed everything for everyone, including animals, plants, and the environment. The industrial revolution started in Great Britain with breakthrough cotton-spinning technology and quickly went viral—spreading to the rest of Europe and North America.

Soon, factories were popping up everywhere, powered by both steam engines and coal. People started making things with iron and steel. Big-time inventions—from artificial lighting to automobiles—changed the way people did business and how we live our lives.

Fast-forward to today, and almost every machine we use was first developed during the industrial revolution. Unfortunately, this progress has come at an environmental cost. Not long after the industrial revolution began, the air became polluted from things like burning coal.

THE SIXTH EXTINCTION

Scientists think the world's gone through five mass extinctions. What's a mass extinction? It happens when at least 75 percent of all species on Earth die off very quickly. (In evolutionary terms, "quick" can be anywhere from thousands to millions of years.)

They've been caused by ice sheets, volcanoes, asteroid strikes (like the one that helped wipe out the dinosaurs), and other environmental shifts, leading to climate change.

Many think we're on the brink of a sixth extinction. Climate change is once again the culprit, but this time it's human caused.

Today's factories pump out more products destined for store shelves than ever before, and we're also creating more pollution than ever, even though some methods of production have gotten cleaner.

This progress has affected a lot of Earth's creatures, but one insect tells the story better than others, and it's become an icon for not-so-natural selection. Most of us only pay attention to this night-flyer when we're camping by candlelight: the moth.

PEPPERED MOTHS

We don't have to go that far back to see how peppered moths became peppered. If we travel to London around 1700—before the industrial revolution—we'd be lucky to spot a peppered moth for two reasons: they were rare and their white wings with black spots blended in perfectly with the lichen-covered bark of the trees they call home.

Like Jandy's neck and Bruno's horn, the color of the peppered moth's wings was probably determined by natural selection. Moths with peppered wings stayed hidden from predators, increasing their survival rate.

If a moth was born with red wings—due to a random mutation that happened at some point—things wouldn't turn out so well. It probably wouldn't survive long enough to have offspring, and the gene mutation that gave the instruction for red would likely die out along with the moth.

CHIM, CHIMNEY

Things changed when Britain started burning coal to fuel its new industrial machines. Soot spewed from smokestacks and drifted through the air. Eventually, it covered everything from buildings to trees.

In the countryside, where peppered moths hang out, trees went from a speckled white-and-black color—created by the combination of light bark and dark lichen—to soot black. White moths with a few dark spots on their wings suddenly stood out like a bad pimple.

This environmental change made the moth easier to be seen by birds, who consider them a perfect afternoon snack.

But then evolution did its thing, and through a random gene mutation, one of these peppered moths—we'll call them Nash—was born with black wings. Nash's friends probably thought Nash was an ugly duckling. And maybe even treated them that way.

But Nash had the last laugh. Since they blended in so well with the soot-covered trees, they lived the longest and probably attracted a mate or two, thanks to those dashing black wings and superhero-like powers of survival.

DID YOU KNOW?

Moths are active during the night; butterflies are active during the day.

The first completely black version of the peppered moth was identified in Britain in 1848, probably several decades after Nash was born—long enough to give their offspring and then their descendants time to reproduce.

Because of Nash and their random gene mutation, black peppered moths thrived. This moth is so common now that there could be one flapping around the light outside your front door.

Your neighborhood moth might be black, but it could also be speckled. Since some of the soot from the industrial revolution has been cleaned up, the peppered look is back in style.

BLENDING IN

Even though the use of coal for energy is decreasing in some countries, human activity still produces a lot of pollution. As we talked about in Chapter Two, climate change is one consequence of this—and it's a big one. Most scientists agree we're currently facing a climate crisis mostly caused by burning fossil fuels that release greenhouse gases (see "Change versus Crisis" on page 28).

This crisis affects different parts of the world in different ways. The trend toward warmer weather has affected tawny owls living in the forests of Finland. Like the peppered moth, they've put on a new coat.

Tawny owls are either brown or pale gray. The cold white winters in Finland have traditionally favored gray owls, which can hide from predators by blending into a snowy backdrop. But as winters have become warmer over the last fifty years, there are fewer gray owls and more brown ones. Why? Brown owls can blend in better with the brown, snow-free branches of the forest.

Another happy not-so-natural selection story, right? Not so fast.

Being brown might help tawny owls survive, but it comes at a cost. Feather color isn't the only genetic difference between the instruction manuals of brown owls and their pale-gray cousins. Brown owls also have weaker immune systems and higher metabolic rates (meaning they need more food), and both are coded in the genes. As the gray-colored owls die out due to lack of snow, so do the genes that might be helpful as disease spreads and food becomes scarcer—both possible outcomes of the climate crisis.

DID YOU KNOW?

There are about 160,000 species of moths and 17,500 species of butterflies.

CHANGING BEHAVIOR

In addition to warmer winters, climate change causes hotter summers and earlier springs. Warmer weather might not sound like a bad thing, but it can take a while for creatures without air-conditioning to adapt.

Insects like the endangered Quino checkerspot butterfly—a tiny fast-flyer that used to be common in California and Mexico—adapt by moving away from the coast and into the hills, where temperatures are cooler. Here, they've learned to survive by laying eggs on different plants.

DID YOU KNOW?

What's the difference between a moth and a butterfly? It's all in the way they rest their wings. Butterflies fold them up, and moths flatten them against their body like a paper airplane.

This may seem like more of a behavioral change than a genetic one, but remember— genes in our instruction manual help determine personality. Problem solving, curiosity, and intelligence are examples of inheritable character traits.

When the clever butterflies move into the hills to escape the heat, they don't go alone. The predators who eat them—other insects, birds, toads, and rats—are forced to go too. All this change can be hard on the ecosystem, which can quickly become overwhelmed by all the new residents. Plants gobbled up by butterfly larvae or by the butterfly's predators may not be strong enough to recover. Things aren't much better for vegetation in areas abandoned by butterflies since there are fewer pollinators around to keep plants healthy.

EVOLUTION UNDER PRESSURE

By blending in with the trees, moths with peppered wings lived longer, healthier lives—allowing them to produce more offspring. When air pollution from the industrial revolution turned those trees black, peppered moths evolved to have black wings through not-so-natural selection.

The moths are fine now, but other creatures, like the tawny owl and the checkerspot butterfly, are still at risk as humans continue to pollute the planet. The climate crisis will increasingly lead to warmer winters, earlier springs, and hotter summers— interrupting evolution and forcing not just individual animals, but also the entire web of life, to adapt to new environments created by us.

Evolution takes time. Most creatures don't have that luxury anymore. Even if they aren't negatively affected by the warming climate, the plants and animals they're connected to might be forced to adapt faster than ever before. In the race to keep up with the pace

of human change through not-so-natural selection, many positive traits—and species—will likely be lost along the way.

We've shown we can do things fast. Now it's time for us to use that speed to protect individual species and the ecosystems that rely on them to maintain diversity and balance on our interconnected planet.

WHAT DO WE DO NOW?

Many countries have limited the burning of coal for energy. Britain, for example, had its first coal-free day in 135 years on April 14, 2017. Coal is still used, though, producing a significant amount of greenhouse gas and contributing to the climate crisis.

Places that don't use coal get energy in other ways—usually from burning other fossil fuels. This is a problem, especially since the world's need for energy is constantly increasing. Just think of how many times you've recharged your devices this week alone.

One way to decrease greenhouse gas emissions is to decrease energy consumption. We all know about the need to reduce gas-powered vehicles, but using less electricity also helps. Some simple, everyday ways people living in developed countries can reduce electricity consumption include

- taking shorter showers (heating water takes lots of energy)
- turning off unneeded lights and using energy-smart bulbs like LEDs
- taking breaks from TV, video games, and computers
- wearing a sweater instead of turning up the heat
- opening a window instead of turning on the air-conditioning
- washing clothes in cold water and hanging them up to dry
- not leaving computers on standby and unplugging devices when they're charged

People don't just use energy at home, of course. Since the industrial revolution, the world's been driven by industry, which includes mining, construction, agriculture, and factories that make everything from paper to smartphones. All of them require energy to do things like

- heat, cool, and ventilate buildings
- operate motors and machinery
- transform raw material into products such as plastics and chemicals
- power lighting, computers, and office equipment

In the United States, factories that manufacture products are responsible for up to 77 percent of industrial energy consumption, meaning a lot of energy is needed to make everyday stuff—even things that don't need to be plugged in, like pencils and flip-flops. And a lot of this energy comes from fossil fuels, including coal.

How can someone who's never stepped foot inside a factory change this? Buy better, so factories don't make so much stuff. What does buying better mean? Think about the following before you head to the store or visit an online merchant:

- Can you fix something that's broken instead of buying a new one?
- Can you buy something used instead of new?
- Is an upgrade to the latest version of your favorite electronic necessary?
- If buying new, is the product made using renewable energy and sustainable materials?

Another way to help is to ask the government to make factories and businesses responsible for their pollution. Write to your local politician expressing your concerns. Many political parties support actions like making factories pay for their pollution and helping companies switch to clean energy.

LOOKING FORWARD

Using less electricity and buying better are good places to start, but they won't solve all our problems because the world's population is getting bigger. And everyone wants stuff that makes their life easier.

The World Energy Council estimates that worldwide about two out of ten people don't have access to any electricity, and most of them want energy to power stuff as much as everyone else. In many cases, the cheapest, easiest way to get it is by burning coal—like we did during the industrial revolution.

While countries around the world are working on reducing their energy use, some countries have been more successful than others. There are many reasons why this might be the case. Everything from a country's wealth and population to its main industries and form of government can impact how a country addresses its use of energy.

As much as we want to reduce energy use overall, none of us want to live without the things most of us take for granted, like heat, lights, and hot water. Looking forward, we need to figure out how to distribute the world's wealth and energy more evenly so everyone has access to modern lifestyle essentials.

Supplying the world with energy *without* burning fossil fuels is key. Clean or renewable energy comes from constantly replenished natural sources. Here are some examples that don't produce pollution:

- Solar cells capture energy from the sun's rays and transform it into energy (see "Solar Ironing Cart").
- Wind produces electricity when it turns the blades of massive turbines.
- Geothermal wells bring heat from Earth's core to the surface.
- Hydroelectric plants convert the force of fast-moving water into electricity (though many feel large hydroelectric plants or mega-dams aren't sustainable because they change the direction and reduce the natural flow of rivers).
- Wave and tidal energy are similar to hydroelectric but rely on the movement of tides.

Getting energy from clean, renewable sources is good for us and the planet: we get the stuff we need without creating so much pollution.

Less pollution won't just help the climate crisis. It will also reduce other forms of air pollution like smog, and both will reduce the impact humans have on Earth and the web of life.

The evolution of many plants and animals was impacted by the industrial revolution, and we've all been forced to adapt to an environment that's rapidly changing. By slowing things down, we'll give our interconnected world a chance to adapt to our growing, modernized population through not-so-natural selection.

SOLAR IRONING CART

In India, people go door-to-door collecting washed clothes that need ironing. They use pushcarts as ironing boards, pressing clothes with a heavy hollow brass iron heated by charcoal burning inside.

Vinisha Umashankar—a high school student from Tiruvannamalai, India—first became concerned about coal-powered irons at age twelve when she noticed ironing vendors dumping burnt charcoal into the garbage. After doing some research, she learned that in many parts of the world, charcoal is made by cutting down trees and burning them. "The use of charcoal pollutes the land, water, and air, reduces the habitats of animals, birds, and insects, decreases agriculture production, intensifies climate change, and magnifies global warming worldwide."

She quickly realized sunshine was the solution. With a little research, she figured out that the number of sunny days in India (more than 300 a year) produced more energy than the country consumed—a lot more. "Using solar energy can also help to cut fossil fuel use, reduce pollution, save Mother Nature, protect the environment, preserve ecosystems, and save a lot of money!"

Vinisha has won many awards, including the international Children's Climate Prize in 2020. Now she's hoping to see solar power replace coal in the more than ten million carts currently used in India. "Each burn about 5 kg (11 pounds) of charcoal every day. That's about 50 million kg (110 million pounds) of charcoal," she says. "Just imagine the irreversible damage it does to the environment."

She has ten other inventions currently getting patented, including a solar mosquito killer and a smart ceiling fan. Her inventions focus on helping the environment or the less privileged. "All of us should understand environmental issues are real, they can't be fixed at a later date, and importantly, they are not someone else's problem. We should work together and understand, plan, and solve environmental issues—before it's too late."

CHAPTER FIVE:

STICKY FEET: HOW CITIES SHAPE LIZARDS

Remember, we started traveling almost a million years ago. The first kingdoms and empires were settled more than five thousand years ago—once we figured out how to farm. Thanks to the industrial revolution, there were suddenly a lot more of us, and we started moving around even more—this time via big ships and airplanes.

Where did we go this time? To the city. People flocked from the farm to the city in numbers never seen before because they wanted to do two things:

1. Live close to factories where they could earn a decent income.
2. Enjoy the "perks" of plumbing and electricity, still rare in rural areas.

In 1910, only about two out of ten people lived in cities. By 2007, more than half the world's population had gone urban. The numbers vary by country. The urban population in Canada, for example, was around 80 percent in 2016—up from 37 percent in 1901.

This migration isn't slowing down. City populations around the world are getting bigger all the time.

CITY SLICKERS

Our move to the city had a big impact on plants and animals still working with the long timelines associated with biological evolution. It takes many generations of trial and error for random genetic mutations to make a species better able to survive, but the creatures we share Earth with didn't have that kind of time because things were changing so fast.

Luckily, evolution in the city happens faster—just like everything else—since city climates are extreme environments with things like

- urban heat islands
- pollution
- noise
- artificial lights
- concrete

In the city, if you don't change, you die!

Cities also have barriers like highways that can divide populations into subgroups. Unlike their wild cousins, these small subgroups have limited options for everything from food to mating partners.

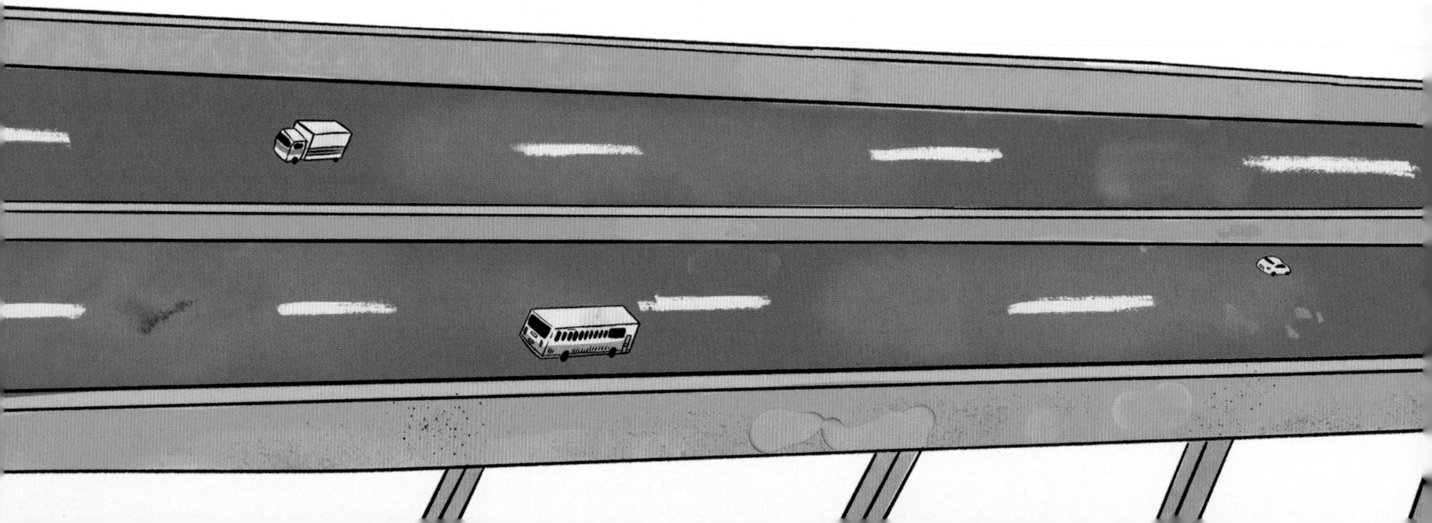

It's like not being able to leave your classroom. Even though there's a water fountain just down the hall, you're not allowed to drink from it. And even though lots of nice kids are in the school, you can only be friends with your classmates.

Scientists—starting with Charles Darwin and Alfred Wallace— have shown that when small, isolated populations live in extreme conditions, evolution speeds up.

If a random gene mutation helps a creature survive in a very challenging environment—where there's extreme heat or limited food, for example—it's like winning the lottery. That creature will pass on the mutation that made it easier for them to survive very quickly because the population is small. And if the creatures that didn't inherit the gene mutation from the one who did die off, only those with the mutation will remain. With this new trait—a survival superpower in that environment—a whole new species could branch off the evolutionary tree.

That's what happened to the birds and lizards Darwin studied on the Galápagos Islands. It also happened to another crafty lizard that adjusted to city life by becoming a distinct species with its own unique urban superpowers: a little lizard from the Caribbean.

STICKY FEET

If you've visited a tropical island, you've probably seen a lizard clinging to the side of a building. You may have even seen them in their natural habitat too—climbing up trees and rocks and waiting there until a snack-sized insect flies or crawls by.

Crested anole lizards, native to the Caribbean islands, are natural climbers known for perching head down on tree trunks. Their superpower comes from their toe pads, which have unique scales—like folded flaps of skin—that make their feet very big when spread out. Each of these scales has tons of very tiny hairs that interact at a microscopic level with whatever surface they come in contact with—a bit like two pieces of Velcro hooking together.

It might sound like magic—or remind you of something from a Spider-Man movie—but now you can probably guess where those tiny hairs came from: natural selection!

DID YOU KNOW?

There are 250 species of anole lizards ranging in color from green or turquoise to gray or brown patterned.

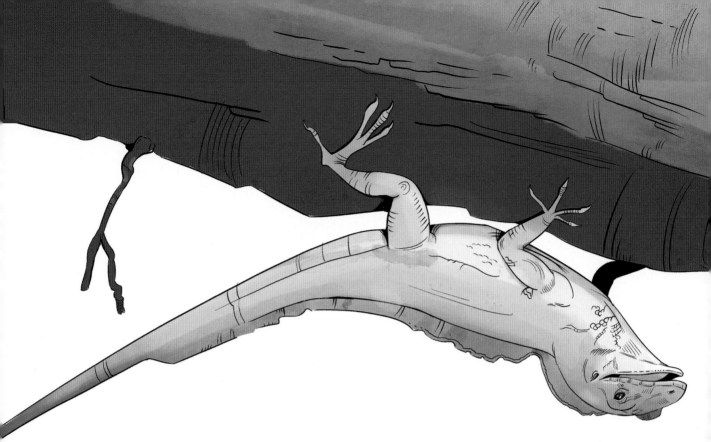

The first lizards born with these extra hairs had an advantage: they could get to areas of the forest other lizards couldn't. Compared to their ancestors, the hairy-toed lizards could easily escape from predators and enjoy access to an all-you-can-eat buffet afterward.

In the forest, too many hairs could mean too much cling, making some getaways tough. At some point in history, natural selection probably determined how many hairs were too much, too little, then just right.

Everything in the Caribbean was "just right" for the anole lizard until the city next to their rain-forest home started spreading into their backyard. Some lizards went urban and found themselves living in San Juan—the biggest city in Puerto Rico.

FROM TREES TO GLASS

In a short time period, trees and rocks were replaced with buildings and roads, and anole lizards had very few trees and rocks to cling to. They had to quickly adapt to smoother surfaces like concrete and glass.

Recently, scientists studying anole lizards have figured out how they did it. Comparing urban lizards to their forest friends, scientists found that city lizards have bigger toe pads with more scales covered even more densely with those tiny, magical hairs.

To test whether these "new-and-improved" feet allowed city lizards to run better on smooth surfaces, scientists set up an experiment where lizards raced up tracks made of metal, painted concrete, and bark. Their conclusion? What was too many hairs for a forest lizard was just right for a city lizard.

Now scientists are trying to determine just how fast this change happened. The lizards they've studied have only been in the city for thirty to forty years. In evolutionary terms, that's less than the blink of an eye.

But for the crested anole—which starts reproducing at just eight months old and keeps doing it all year long for its entire life—it's enough time to produce a hundred new generations. And since city lizards have limited mating options when they first arrive in town, the genes associated with big, scaly, hairy feet got passed on relatively quickly.

BEATING THE HEAT

More recently, the anole lizard has developed another not-so-natural superpower: adapting to city climate change.

Unlike the tawny owl, the lizard hasn't changed color—although anoles do come in an impressive variety of colors and designs. Instead, they've changed the way their body handles heat.

Compared with larger toe pads and specialized scales, beating the heat is a complex trait controlled by many different genes. For a tiny creature like the anole lizard—smaller than your palm from nose to tail—it's an even bigger challenge. Especially since they're cold blooded, meaning their body temperature is determined by the air temperature.

Luckily, the San Juan lizards have been in a climate crisis boot camp. In the instruction manual of lizards that grew up in Puerto Rican urban heat islands (see sidebar), there's one specific DNA change in a gene that appears to "turn on" when the critter's exposed to heat. Genes that turn on and off are like sections in an instruction manual that only get read under certain conditions.

When the heat goes up and the gene turns on, it sends a signal to a bunch of other genes. We don't yet know what genes the signal targets, but it probably says something like "Thermal tolerance—activate!"

Scientists refer to this trait as "plasticity"—a creature's ability to be flexible in responding to its environment. Plasticity occurs in many living things from plants that grow bigger leaves in the shade so they can capture more light to butterflies with wings that change color and pattern in different seasons to help them hide from predators.

Lizards with the plasticity trait can function at temperatures about 1 °C (1.8 °F) warmer than their less flexible forest-dwelling mates, allowing them to go about their business in temperatures greater than 40 °C (104 °F). These lizards can stay active longer, giving them more time to gather food. And they can perch in places exposed to more heat, so they have more spaces for hunting, sleeping, and mating.

The plasticity trait will give anole lizards a big advantage as temperatures rise in response to the climate crisis, especially since cities are projected to get hotter and food and habitat more limited.

URBAN HEAT ISLANDS

Urban heat islands—sounds good, right? Unfortunately, we're not talking about tropical paradises.

Urban heat islands are big, busy city areas that are much hotter than surrounding rural areas. Turning up the heat are things like

- people
- cars, buses, and trains
- houses, shops, and industrial buildings built close together

The city of Las Vegas, for example, can get up to 13 °C (24 °F) hotter than rural areas. This is hard on plants and animals and can cause health problems for people, like heatstroke and exposure to dangerous levels of air pollution.

PESKY PETS

Luckily, tourists seem to love these city lizards. And since they eat annoying insects, locals like them too.

Other city animals aren't so lucky. Take mice, for example.

The white-footed mice of New York City don't care that most of us scream and jump on a chair when someone spots them. The mice want to live in New York, New York, as much as the over eight million people they share it with. Or maybe they don't have a choice—they lived there long before it was covered with skyscrapers and subways.

As the city has grown up around them, the habitat of the white-footed mouse has become limited to little islands of green surrounded by concrete and traffic. It's hard for mice to come and go from their small island, so they've become an isolated population.

One specific family of mice—we'll call them the Central Parkers—has evolved through not-so-natural selection in a way that might make you jealous: they can eat very fatty foods without getting a stomachache. Why would this give them an advantage? They can eat the greasy snacks left behind by people whose eyes were bigger than their stomachs.

Central Parkers have also become good at tolerating toxic metals in the soil. This allows them to eat their more natural diet of grass, acorns, and tree nuts grown in polluted city soil. This is good for Central Parkers but potentially bad for us: if a mouse can tolerate toxins, it can also survive eating poison.

You might not like the idea of poisoning Central Parkers, but it can be necessary in an urban environment loaded with mice—especially since they often carry disease. If regular poison can't take care of an infestation, we're forced to use even more toxic potions. If mice evolve to tolerate these stronger poisons, then the cycle continues.

DID YOU KNOW?

Community scientists in the Netherlands collected photos of European snails using an app called Snail Snap to help study the hypothesis that snails living in urban heat islands have lighter colored shells because dark colors absorb more heat than light ones.

EVOLUTION UNDER PRESSURE

How sticky lizards' feet are depends on where they live. Thanks to natural selection, forest lizards have not-so-sticky feet, so they can cling to trees without getting stuck. Thanks to not-so-natural selection, city lizards have much stickier feet, so they can cling to buildings made of concrete and glass.

Anole lizards in Puerto Rico have also adjusted to living in hotter cities through plasticity. Heat turns on a gene in their instruction manual that triggers a response. Like a set of falling dominoes, a set of genes that can help the lizard beat the heat gets turned on by that first gene.

Mice have also responded to city life through not-so-natural selection. A change in their digestive instruction manual allows them to eat unhealthy human food and tolerate poison—superpowers that help other city pests survive too.

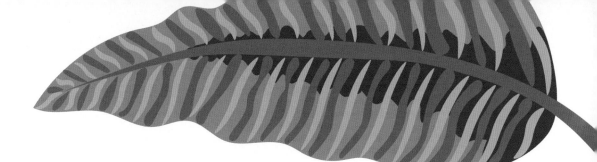

In the city, humans are creating a whole new web of life. This might not seem like a bad thing. But given how quickly cities change, this web is easily broken. Plants and animals that have adapted to the not-so-natural city life could be out of luck if they ever try to move back to the country, which could happen if all the green islands disappear.

WHAT DO WE DO NOW?

Going urban has been good for humans because it's given us so much control over our environment. It's happened so quickly, though, that even humans have struggled to adapt to big city life. Extreme heat, pollution, noise, and artificial lights aren't exactly good for our health.

Some plants and animals have evolved shockingly fast to the extreme habitats we've created. But it hasn't happened without risk of scary-sounding things like invasion, infestation, and toxic tolerance. Plus, there's a limit to how fast any creature can evolve—even those that reproduce quickly.

One way we can make cities better for everyone is by "going green." Here, we're actually talking about becoming the color green—covered with vegetation. Green spaces provide habitat and food for animals. Trees and plants help filter city air, making it cleaner for everyone. As they gobble up carbon dioxide—one of the biggest greenhouse gases produced from burning fossil fuels for energy—they send out oxygen and help reduce climate change.

Cities around the world are going green in different ways:

- **Tokyo, Japan**, converted a large landfill in Tokyo Bay into Umino-Mori (Sea Forest) by covering the garbage with soil left over from construction projects, topping it with compost, and planting thousands of trees. If you watched the 2020 Summer Olympics held in Japan, you might have seen athletes competing in the Sea Forest Waterway, a rowing course built next to the converted landfill.
- The world's first vertical urban forest, Bosco Verticale, was built in **Milan, Italy**. The apartment complex has two tall towers with seven hundred trees, five thousand shrubs, and eleven thousand smaller plants growing from ladder-like balconies that run all the way to the top. The city is planning more green buildings covered in living walls and solar panels.
- Way before it was trendy, **Curitiba, Brazil**, closed six city blocks to cars and made public parks a priority.
- **Toronto, Ontario**, was the first city in North America to pass a green roof law that requires plants to be grown on the roofs of big, new buildings, like McNicoll Bus Garage, which is half covered in drought-tolerant plants.

City planners, architects, and politicians need to create more green spaces as urbanization continues. There are several ways you can help too:

Rethink your lawn

A traditional grass lawn isn't great for city ecosystems because people use a lot of pesticides to keep them weed free and a lot of water and fertilizer to keep them alive.

Native grasses and trees are a better option and should grow well in the soil you have with the amount of natural rainfall you get, providing a good habitat for city critters.

DID YOU KNOW?

The Florida Wildlife Corridor—a network of protected habitat on public and private land—is helping protect panthers from many dangers, including hunters and highways.

Make a habitat garden

Convincing your parent or landlord to rip out the lawn and start over might be difficult. But maybe there's a small space around your home you can convert to a habitat garden, which can be as simple as one native plant, a rock, and a piece of wood. Native plants can provide food for birds and insects (see "No Mow May" on page 101). Plants—along with rocks and wood—can also offer shelter to insects, worms, and salamanders.

Plant a vegetable garden

By growing things you like to eat, you might end up sharing your harvest with urban wildlife. But that's a lot better for them than leftover junk food or garbage!

Tight on space? Some vegetables and herbs can grow well in a balcony pot or window box. Or you and some friends could rent a community garden plot. If your city doesn't have a community garden, talk to your local government about creating one.

LOOKING FORWARD

No matter how green we make the city, plants and animals need space—like we sometimes need space from our friends and family. But here, we're talking about space away from everything human.

A small strip of human-free greenery can make a big difference. Just ask the animals who live in Banff, a national park in Alberta, Canada, that welcomes over 3.5 million human visitors every year—not including the millions who drive through on the Trans-Canada Highway without stopping.

To keep asphalt and animals from mixing, fences were put up along this highway. But animals still wanted to cross. Who could blame them? Anything from dinner to the love of their life could be on the other side of the fenced freeway.

The solution? Wildlife bridges give animals a way to cross busy roads without becoming roadkill.

Since the first wildlife bridge was built in Banff over twenty years ago, car collisions with bears, cougars, elk, and other animals have decreased by more than 80 percent. Six overpasses and thirty-eight underpasses are now situated along the Trans-Canada, inspiring other places to also build them.

Corridors of grass, trees, and wildflowers like these allow animal species to move freely from one area to another, preventing them from being divided into small subgroups and allowing them to find new sources of food, water, and mates. All these things increase their likelihood of survival and decrease their need to rapidly evolve in response to not-so-natural selection.

In Chapter Four, we talked about the Quino checkerspot butterfly adapting to climate change by moving to the hills. Unfortunately, this may be a temporary solution. The Quino's habitat is still under threat from agricultural and urban development: more than 75 percent of its range has been lost to development and its population has declined by more than 95 percent. For these small butterflies afraid of heights, border walls could block their path to survival.

As cities expand, we must encourage people in charge of land-use planning and management to make decisions with plants and animals in mind. We also need to support architects, developers, and governments who want to conserve wild spaces, build green corridors, and make cities more welcoming for the animals, plants, and people who live there.

If we don't, we could be interrupting the evolution of many more creatures and pushing the world's ecosystem completely out of balance. No one wants to see the planet turned into one giant city. Even those of us who live an urban life need to escape into nature every once in a while.

Perhaps even more importantly, we still need land to grow our crops. And no matter how much we try to control agriculture, we still rely on creatures like insects and birds to pollinate the plants.

We've seen how animals can adapt to human activity through not-so-natural selection. No matter what we do, all creatures must continue to change and evolve, whether by the natural environment or the human-made one. But we can definitely make it easier for them to do it.

Even though cities may be built for humans, it's important that we consider how plants and animals fit into them. Otherwise, we could end up with a world full of only humans, and like a spider without a web, it can't survive very long.

MAKING A DIFFERENCE:

NO MOW MAY

To improve city green space, the Nature Conservancy—which aims to create a world where people and nature thrive together—encourages No Mow May. The idea is simple (and could even get you out of doing some chores!).

When you take a break from mowing the lawn, flowers—including the kinds some people think of as weeds, like dandelions—bloom. This provides an important source of nectar and pollen for wild bees, butterflies, and other pollinating insects, improving habitats for native pollinators, migratory birds, and other wildlife like frogs.

University student Allyson Carroll—an intern at Nature Conservancy Canada—is passionate about ditching the lawn mower. "I love the No Mow May campaign! It's incredibly important to conserve habitat for all species, even the tiny ones that some people don't normally think of when talking about conservation. Throughout my education I've learned how easily an ecosystem can be disrupted by the loss of a single species, so I'm very excited to see residents engaging in this initiative!"

Another university student—Aadya Joshi, originally from Mumbai, India—

is doing something similar through The Right Green, which helps people choose native plants to create biodiversity-rich ecosystems within cities.

After getting permission to clean up a junkyard of a nearby police station in her neighborhood when she was fifteen, Aadya and her brother found something interesting while searching for a lost cricket ball: "In the undergrowth (beneath abandoned cars and garbage) were remnants of a garden amidst piles of rusting metal," Aadya explains.

With help from volunteers, Aadya got to work. "It was incredible to witness how, just months later, a beautiful biodiversity garden with butterflies and birds emerged. Best of all, a fragmented community came together with a new garden as its heart."

Aadya also learned about soil restoration and the plant-insect relationship. To share this knowledge, she developed the BioPower Index, a collection of identification guides on native plants, butterflies, and birds that became part of The Right Green, which also provides workshops and school programs.

CONCLUSION

Natural selection and random gene mutation are the two key forces in determining how creatures evolve and adapt to their natural environment. Over the past century, however, humans have taken over for Mother Nature. Not-so-natural selection (the way animals adapt to us) and genetic manipulation (our ability to change the instruction manual through biotechnology like gene editing) are now responsible for determining which plants and animals live and die.

In this book, we've explained natural versus not-so-natural, but it's important to remember the line between the two is blurry. What might have started out as a natural occurrence—like wildfire—can quickly become unnatural when humans get involved.

There's no line between us and the rest of the creatures that have branched off the evolutionary tree. We all evolved from the same ancestor and live on the same planet. What happens to plants and animals alters human beings just as human activity alters plants and animals—because we are all interconnected in the web of life.

This book has focused on the creatures who survived—and even thrived—thanks to not-so-natural selection. There are many plants and animals that haven't been so lucky. In fact, scientists estimate that up to 150 species go extinct every day.

Our own evolution isn't driven by biological changes created through random genetic mutation and natural selection anymore, either. Instead, human evolution is largely driven by the things we've learned, the systems we've created, and the stuff we've made.

As we've evolved, our impact on the environment has increased and so has the speed of change. Our ancestors survived through hunting and gathering for millions of years before moving to the farm. After thousands of years on the farm, we figured out how to use engines and machines. This led to the industrial revolution, which over a few hundred years has resulted in mass urbanization.

As humans, we need to make sure we're not moving so fast that we can't adapt to our own self-made environment. We also need to make sure that we don't leave anyone behind. Just like plants and animals, the human species needs diversity—which includes different cultures and different ways of life—in order to survive.

Moving forward, humans must make decisions about things like hunting, agricultural practices, technology, and land use by asking ourselves important questions such as

- What purpose does the activity serve for humans?
- What impact does the activity have on other animals, plants, and microorganisms?
- What effect will this have on Earth's entire ecosystem?

Not-so-natural selection shows us that nature—everything from microbes to plants to animals to us—is resilient. But we've never had to adapt to change as fast as we do today. And we don't know how the web of life will respond in the future.

Humans aren't going to stop progressing. We will continue to have a large impact on the world, and it's up to us whether that impact is positive or not so positive. It's important to slow down, recognize our spot in the web of life, and take our role as the driver of evolution seriously. Our fellow creatures are relying on us.

ACKNOWLEDGMENTS

I wrote this book from my home in Rossland, British Columbia, at the base of Red Mountain. The original inhabitants of this area—the Sinixt Arrow Lakes People (or sngaytskstx)—referred to the mountain as kmarkn. Sinixt People came to kmarkn to gather huckleberries during the summer months. I am privileged to work, live, and play in the traditional territories of the Sinixt People.

Evolution Under Pressure started as a pitch to the BC Arts Council with the title *Not-So-Natural Selection: Tangelos, Micropigs, and Wolphins*. The funding I received through their Project Assistance: Creative Writers allowed my original idea to evolve into something that I hope will have a profound impact on the way people interact with the complex web of life.

Thank you to Kaela Cadieux, who took a good idea and turned it into something great. With patience, persistence, and profound insight, you helped me say what I really wanted to say. I'm very proud of this book we created together. You're a great editor—I'm lucky to have you not just as a colleague but also as a friend.

To the entire team at Annick, thank you for making books that nourish young people and cultivate their greatness. It's been an honor to work with you all on this book and since I believe in the magic of three, I really hope we can work on another book soon.

Deep gratitude to those who agreed to be interviewed for this book: Aadya Joshi, Allyson Carroll, Kayla White, Tanya Ball, and Vinisha Umshankar. You all inspire me to do more and give me confidence in the next generation. To everyone who's working to improve our relationship with nature and make the world a better place—thank you.

The older I get, the more my relationships evolve—not just with the planet but also with the people on it. I'm lucky to have many family, friends, and fellow writers who both support and challenge me to do better. To name just a few: Heather Martin, Kyra Martin, Mae Demartin, Ellen Luft, John Luft, Denine Brownlee, Mari Conradi, Christine Thomas Alderman, Samika Swift, Jerry Mikorenda, Miriam Spitzer, and Rosa Jordan.

Then there are those I share my life with day-to-day. Thank you to Oliver and Spencer, who've changed me in ways so profound I can't even describe them (and I'm a writer!). Never stop being exactly who you are and want to be. And Tim, thank you for being my partner in everything. I love being on this journey with you.

RESOURCES

Berkley University of California. "Natural Selection: Charles Darwin and Alfred Russel Wallace." The History of Evolutionary Thought. May 19, 2022. https://evolution.berkeley.edu/evolibrary/article/0_0_0/history_14.

Biello, David. "Will Organic Food Fail to Feed the World?" *Scientific American*. April 25, 2012. https://www.scientificamerican.com/article/organic-farming-yields-and-feeding-the-world-under-climate-change/.

Blakemore, Erin. "New Evidence Shows Peppered Moths Changed Color in Sync with the Industrial Revolution." *Smithsonian Magazine*. June 1, 2016. https://www.smithsonianmag.com/smart-news/new-evidence-peppered-moths-changed-color-sync-industrial-revolution-180959282/.

Bradford, Alina. "Facts About Rhinos." LiveScience. March 20, 2018. https://www.livescience.com/27439-rhinos.html.

Bradford, Alina. "Pigs, Hogs & Boars: Facts About Swine." LiveScience. October 5, 2018. https://www.livescience.com/50623-pigs-facts.html.

Brennand, Emma. "Owls Change Colour as Climate Warms." *Earth News*. February 22, 2011. http://news.bbc.co.uk/earth/hi/earth_news/newsid_9401000/9401733.stm.

Caira, Simonetta, et al. "Innovation for Sustainable Agriculture and Food Production." *Reference Module in Food Science* (2016). https://doi.org/10.1016/B978-0-08-100596-5.21018-4.

Camerlink, Irene, et al. "Tail Postures and Tail Motion in Pigs: A Review." *Applied Animal Behaviour Science* 230 (September 2020): 105079. https://www.sciencedirect.com/science/article/pii/S0168159120301672.

Campbell-Staton, Shane C., et al. "Parallel Selection on Thermal Physiology Facilitates Repeated Adaptation of City Lizards to Urban Heat Islands." *Nature Ecology & Evolution*, no. 4 (March 2020): 652—658. https://doi.org/10.1038/s41559-020-1131-8.

Chapman, Robert. "Are We Really Prepared for the Genetic Revolution?" *Scientific American*. May 27, 2018. https://www.scientificamerican.com/article/are-we-really-prepared-for-the-genetic-revolution/.

Christ, Costas. "Bright Lights, Big Cities Going Green." *National Geographic*. July 18, 2013. https://www.nationalgeographic.com/travel/article/bright-lights-big-cities-going-green.

City of Toronto. "City of Toronto Green Roof Bylaw." May 19, 2022. https://www.toronto.ca/city-government/planning-development/official-plan-guidelines/green-roofs/green-roof-bylaw/.

Coghlan, Andy. "Colourful Pigs Evolved Through Farming, Not Nature." New Scientist. January 16, 2009. https://www.newscientist.com/article/dn16427-colourful-pigs-evolved-through-farming-not-nature/.

Cox, Sarah. "Meet the Kaska Land Guardians. The Narwhal." Kaska Dena Council. September 4, 2019. https://kaskadenacouncil.com/meet-the-kaska-land-guardians-the-narwhal/.

Diamond, Jared. *Guns, Germs, and Steel*. New York: W. W. Norton, 1999.

Dickie, Gloria. "As Banff's Famed Wildlife Overpasses Turn 20, the World Looks to Canada for Conservation Inspiration." *Canadian Geographic*. December 4, 2017. https://www.canadiangeographic.ca/article/banffs-famed-wildlife-overpasses-turn-20-world-looks-canada-conservation-inspiration.

Dobney, Keith. "How Did Wild Boar Become Farmyard Pigs? Genetic Data Reveals the Answer." *The Conversation*. September 1, 2015. https://theconversation.com/how-did-wild-boar-become-farmyard-pigs-genetic-data-reveals-the-answer-46907.

Drake, Nadia. "Will Humans Survive the Sixth Great Extinction?" *National Geographic*. June 23, 2015. https://www.nationalgeographic.com/adventure/article/150623-sixth-extinction-kolbert-animals-conservation-science-world.

Enriquez, Juan, and Steven Gullans. *Evolving Ourselves: How Unnatural Selection and Nonrandom Mutation Are Changing Life on Earth*. New York: Penguin, 2015.

Frangoul, Anmar. "Milan's Skyline Set for Another 'Mutant Building' Covered in Plants." *CNBC*. February 11, 2021. https://www.cnbc.com/2021/02/11/milans-skyline-to-add-another-mutant-building-covered-in-plants-.html.

Greenwald, Noah, et al. *A Wall in the Wild: The Disastrous Impacts of Trump's Border Wall on Wildlife*. Center for Biological Diversity. May 2017. https://www.biologicaldiversity.org/programs/international/borderlands_and_boundary_waters/pdfs/A_Wall_in_the_Wild.pdf.

Gut, Larry, et al. "How Pesticide Resistance Develops." Michigan State University. May 19, 2022. https://www.canr.msu.edu/grapes/integrated_pest_management/how-pesticide-resistance-develops.

Harari, Yuval Noah. *Sapiens: A Brief History of Humankind*. New York: Harper, 2015.

Harris, S. E., et al. "Signatures of Positive Selection and Local Adaptation to Urbanization in White-Footed Mice *(Peromyscus leucopus)*." *Molecular Ecology* 26, no. 22 (October 2017): 6336—6350. https://doi.org/10.1111/mec.14369.

Hirst, K. Kris. "Animal Domestication - Table of Dates and Places." ThoughtCo. January 27, 2019. https://www.thoughtco.com/animal-domestication-table-dates-places-170675.

Hirst, K. Kris. "The Domestication of Pigs: *Sus Scrofa*'s Two Distinct Histories." ThoughtCo. July 3, 2019. https://www.thoughtco.com/the-domestication-of-pigs-170665.

Hunter, Philip. "Genomics Yields Fresh Insights on Plant Domestication." *EMBO Reports* 19, no. 11 (November 2018): e47153. https://doi.org/10.15252/embr.201847153.

Jachmann, P. S., et al. "Tusklessness in African Elephants: A Future Trend." *African Journal of Ecology* 33, no. 3 (September 1995): 230—235. https://doi.org/10.1111/j.1365-2028.1995.tb00800.x

Jambeck, Jenna R., et al. "Plastic Waste Inputs from Land into the Ocean." *Science* 347, no. 6223 (February 2015): 768—771. https://www.science.org/doi/10.1126/science.1260352.

Karell, P., et al. "Climate Change Drives Microevolution in a Wild Bird." *Nature Communications* 2 (February 2011): 208. https://doi.org/10.1038/ncomms1213.

Klappenbach, Laura. "London's Peppered Moths." ThoughtCo. March 31, 2019. https://www.thoughtco.com/londons-peppered-moths-128999.

Le Page, Michael. "Unnatural Selection: Hunting Down Elephants' Tusks." New Scientist. April 27, 2011. https://www.newscientist.com/article/mg21028101-900-unnatural-selection-hunting-down-elephants-tusks/.

Le Page, Michael. "Unnatural Selection: Living with Pollution." New Scientist. April 27, 2011. https://www.newscientist.com/article/mg21028102-300-unnatural-selection-living-with-pollution/.

Liu, L., et al. "Enhancing Grain-Yield-Related Traits by CRISPR—Cas9 Promoter Editing of Maize CLE Genes." Nature Plants 7 (February 2021): 287—294. https://doi.org/10.1038/s41477-021-00858-5.

Losos, Jonathan B., et al. "Evolutionary Implications of Phenotypic Plasticity in the Hindlimb of the Lizard Anolis Sagrei." Evolution 54, no. 1 (February 2000): 301—305. https://doi.org/10.1111/j.0014-3820.2000.tb00032.x.

Main, Douglas. "How America's Most Endangered Cat Could Help Save Florida." National Geographic. March 9, 2021. https://www.nationalgeographic.com/magazine/article/florida-panthers-return-imperiled-by-development-feature.

Maisels, Fiona, et al. "Devastating Decline of Forest Elephants in Central Africa." PLOS ONE 8, no. 3 (March 2013): e59469. https://doi.org/10.1371/journal.pone.0059469.

Marino, Lori, et al. "Thinking Pigs: A Comparative Review of Cognition, Emotion, and Personality in Sus domesticus." International Journal of Comparative Psychology 28 (2015). https://escholarship.org/uc/item/8sx4s79c.

Marris, Emma. "How a Few Species Are Hacking Climate Change." National Geographic. May 6, 2014. https://www.nationalgeographic.com/science/article/140506-climate-change-adaptation-evolution-coral-science-butterflies.

Newman, Matthew. "Swine Domestication aka 'The Pig Porkification Project.'" 4-H Animal Science Resource Blog. March 15, 2019. https://4hanimalscience.rutgers.edu/2019/03/15/1747/.

Norwich University Online. "The Most Important Developments in Human History." October 6, 2020. https://online.norwich.edu/academic-programs/masters/history/resources/infographics/the-most-important-developments-in-human-history.

Nuwer, Rachel. "Here's What Might Happen to Local Ecosystems If All the Rhinos Disappear." Smithsonian Magazine. February 27, 2014. https://www.smithsonianmag.com/articles/heres-what-might-happen-local-ecosystems-if-all-rhinos-disappear-180949896/.

O'Grady, Cathleen. "The Price of Protecting Rhinos." The Atlantic. January 13, 2020. https://www.theatlantic.com/science/archive/2020/01/war-rhino-poaching/604801/.

Palumbi, Stephen R. "Humans as the World's Greatest Evolutionary Force." Science Magazine. September 7, 2001. https://www.science.org/doi/10.1126/science.293.5536.1786.

Panos, Evangelos, et al. "Access to Electricity in the World Energy Council's Global Energy Scenarios: An Outlook for Developing Regions Until 2030." *Energy Strategy Reviews* 9 (March 2016): 28—49. https://doi.org/10.1016/j.esr.2015.11.003.

Parmesan, C., et al. "Endangered Quino Checkerspot Butterfly and Climate Change: Short-Term Success but Long-Term Vulnerability?" *Journal of Insect Conservation* 19 (December 2014): 185—204. https://doi.org/10.1007/s10841-014-9743-4.

PBS Nature. "Rhino Horn Use: Fact vs. Fiction." August 20, 2010. https://www.pbs.org/wnet/nature/rhinoceros-rhino-horn-use-fact-vs-fiction/1178/.

Pearce, Fred. "Global Extinction Rates: Why Do Estimates Vary So Wildly?" *Yale Environment* 360. August 17, 2015. https://e360.yale.edu/features/global_extinction_rates_why_do_estimates_vary_so_wildly.

Potts, Rick. "Introduction to Human Evolution." Smithsonian. February 3, 2022. http://humanorigins.si.edu/education/introduction-human-evolution.

Redding, Richard, et al. "Ancestral Pigs: A New (Guinea) Model for Pig Domestication in the Middle East." *Ancestors for the Pigs: Pigs in Prehistory* 15 (1998): 65—76.

Reference. "Why Do Pigs Have Curly Tails?" March 28, 2020. https://www.reference.com/pets-animals/pigs-curly-tails-f0ba14c9fee9b461.

Regalado, Antonio. "Gene Editing Has Made Pigs Immune to a Deadly Epidemic." *MIT Technology Review*. December 11, 2020. https://www.technologyreview.com/2020/12/11/1013176/crispr-pigs-prrs-cd163-genus/.

Schilthuizen, Menno. *Darwin Comes to Town: How the Urban Jungle Drives Evolution*. London: Picador, 2018.

Scoville, Heather. "How Artificial Selection Works with Animals." ThoughtCo. September 29, 2021. https://www.thoughtco.com/artificial-selection-in-animals-1224592.

Shinn, Lora. "Renewable Energy: The Clean Facts." NRDC. June 15, 2018. https://www.nrdc.org/stories/renewable-energy-clean-facts.

Statistics Canada. "2016 Census: 150 Years of Urbanization in Canada." February 8, 2017. https://www.statcan.gc.ca/en/sc/video/2016census_150yearsurbanization.

Statistics Canada. "Proportion of the Canadian Population Living in Urban Regions Since 1901." September 22, 2009. https://www12.statcan.gc.ca/census-recensement/2006/as-sa/97-550/figures/c5-eng.cfm.

Tarlach, Gemma. "The Five Mass Extinctions That Have Swept Our Planet." *Discover.* July 18, 2018. https://www.discovermagazine.com/the-sciences/mass-extinctions.

Tokyo Metropolitan Government. "Creation of Beautiful, Elegant Cityscapes." Bureau of Urban Development. May 19, 2022. https://www.metro.tokyo.lg.jp/english/about/tech/documents/05_p99-p135_1.pdf.

University of Queensland. "Hotter, Drier, CRISPR: Editing for Climate Change." *ScienceDaily.* March 1, 2021. https://www.sciencedaily.com/releases/2021/03/210301112331.htm.

U.S. Energy Information Administration. "Use of Energy Explained: Energy Use in Industry." August 2, 2021. https://www.eia.gov/energyexplained/use-of-energy/industry.php.

U.S. Fish and Wildlife Service. *Facts about Rhino Horn.* Office of Law Enforcement. May 19, 2022. https://medisf.traasgpu.com/mfis/34e20b34163e13dd.pdf.

van der Burg, Karin R. L., et al. "Seasonal Plasticity: How Do Butterfly Wing Pattern Traits Evolve Environmental Responsiveness?" *Current Opinion in Genetics & Development 69* (August 2021): 82—87. https://doi.org/10.1016/j.gde.2021.02.009.

Washington University in St. Louis. "Hot Time in the City: Urban Lizards Evolve Heat Tolerance." *ScienceDaily.* March 10, 2020. https://www.sciencedaily.com/releases/2020/03/200310094231.htm.

Wilkinson, Freddie. "Industrial Revolution and Technology." *National Geographic.* January 9, 2020. https://www.nationalgeographic.org/article/industrial-revolution-and-technology/.

Winchell, K. M,. et al. "Phenotypic Shifts in Urban Areas in the Tropical Lizard *Anolis cristatellus.*" *Evolution* 70, no. 5 (May 2016): 1009—1022. https://doi.org/10.1111/evo.12925.

Winchell, K. M., et al. "Phylogenetic Signal and Evolutionary Correlates of Urban Tolerance in a Widespread Neotropical Lizard Clade." *Evolution* 74, no. 7 (July 2020): 1274—1288. https://doi.org/10.1111/evo.13947.

Worrall, Simon. "In Cities, Wildlife Evolves Astonishingly Fast." *National Geographic.* May 4, 2018. https://www.nationalgeographic.com/science/articleurban-living-drives-evolution-in-surprising-way.

FOR MORE INFORMATION

Carbon Brief: Global Coal Power

https://www.carbonbrief.org/
mapped-worlds-coal-power-plants

Khan Academy: The Industrial Revolution

https://www.khanacademy.org/
humanities/big-history-project/acceleration/
bhp-acceleration/a/the-industrial-revolution

Kurzgesagt — In a Nutshell Video: What Happened Before History? Human Origins.

https://www.youtube.com/watch?v=
dGiQaabX3_o

Rhino Rescue Project

http://rhinorescueproject.org

Save the Rhino

https://www.savetherhino.org

Science News for Students: Cities Drive Animals and Plants to Evolve

https://www.sciencenewsforstudents.org/article/
cities-drive-animals-and-plants-evolve

Stuff You Should Know Podcast: What Will Farming 4.0 Look Like?

https://www.happyscribe.com/public/
stuff-you-should-know/what-will-farming-4

Ted Talk: How Animals and Plants Are Evolving in Cities with Menno Schilthuizen

https://www.ted.com/talks/menno_schilthuizen_
how_animals_and_plants_are_evolving_in_cities

Ted Talk: What Explains the Rise of Humans? (by Yuval Noah Harari)

https://www.ted.com/talks/yuval_noah_harari_
what_explains_the_rise_of_humans

MAKING A DIFFERENCE

Children's Climate Prize

https://www.ccprize.org

Grow Dat

https://growdatyouthfarm.org

Indigenous Guardians Toolkit

https://www.indigenousguardianstoolkit.ca

Kaska Dena Council

https://kaskadenacouncil.com

The Pollination Project

https://thepollinationproject.org

The Right Green

https://www.therightgreen.org

Earthshot Prize Video: World Leaders Summit

#COP26 with Vinisha Umashankar

https://www.youtube.com/watch?v=zvLD6waVlkk

INDEX

size of brains, 21, 22

survival of, 19

and upright walking, 21, 22

hunting practices

and animal control, 37—38

effect on human movement, 40

equipment used, 40, 41

of humans, 22

in Kaska Dena First Nations, 39

for moose, 39

responsible, 32

sustainable, 39

I

industrial revolution

effect of, 61, 62

and pollution, 62

J

Joshi, Aadya, 101

L

lawns

alternatives to, 96

no-mowing of, 101

lettuce-bot, 55

lizards. *See* anole lizards

M

mass extinctions, 62

mass production, and industrial revolution, 62, 63

mice

adaptation to urban living, 91

in urban environment, 90—91, 92

moths. *See also* peppered moths

activity period, 66

attraction to light, 65

compared to butterflies, 70

mutations

advantages of, 9

continuing, 10

and gene code, 7

in genes, 8

random nature of, 8

in rhino genes, 24

N

natural selection

in anole lizards, 84, 85

and climate change, 38

and environment, 15

in forest lizards, 92

and giraffe's neck, 13—14

and humans, 17—18

importance of, 102

and peppered moth, 65

and rhino horns, 24

survival of the fittest, 13

theory of, 12—13

and theory of evolution, 2, 16, 102

and warthogs, 47

No Mow May, 101

not-so-natural selection

effect of, 2, 102, 105

and elephants, 31

and gene editing, 52, 56

and humans, 16, 17—18

and lizards, 92

and mice, 91, 92

and owls, 69

and the peppered moth, 63—67, 72

and pig breeding, 44—45, 47

in plants, 50—51

purpose of, 102

and rhino horns, 27

O

organisms, single-cell, 5, 7, 10

P

peppered moths

colour of wings, 64, 65

evolution of wing colour, 66—67, 72

and not-so-natural selection, 63—67, 72

random genetic mutation in, 66, 67

rarity of sighting, 64

pigs. *See also* bacon

breeding of, 44—45

challenge in hunting, 44

changing genes of, 49

choosing for breeding, 45, 46

choosing for eating, 45, 46

eating habits, 44